David Amram, whose many activities include compositions for concerts and plays, movie scores, and classical pieces. (Photo credit: RCA Records)

Barney Bigard, the great jazz clarinetist, for many years a mainstay of the Ellington band. (Photo: Hans Harzheim)

Eubie Blake's resurgence in the early 1970s
heralded new interest in ragtime piano.
(Photo: Ed Lawless)

Donald Byrd has composed, arranged, taught at Howard University, and appears with his own group.

Hoagy Carmichael. Many of his tunes, including *Stardust, Skylark, The Nearness of You,* and *Rockin' Chair,* are perennial favorites with jazzmen. (Photo: Lou Mack)

3

Pianist **Chick Corea's** Return to Forever has been one of the most prominent combos of the 1970s.

Buddy DeFranco brought modern jazz improvisation to the clarinet. In recent years he has led the Glenn Miller Orchestra.

4

Billy Eckstine hosting *The Jazz Show*, KNBC-TV, Los Angeles, 1971.

Mercer Ellington, a talented composer-arranger himself, carries on the great tradition of his father's orchestra.

Dizzy Gillespie, one of the founders of the be-bop revolution in the early 1940s, was the first to tour abroad via a State Department subsidy (1956). His long career continues unabated, with concerts, club dates, and recordings. (Photo: Ulrich Borchert)

Norman Granz with Ella Fitzgerald.
Granz's Jazz at the Philharmonic tours are known
world-wide. He was the first to record live jazz concerts.
(Photo: Phil Stern)

Herbie Hancock, the bright
alumnus of the Miles Davis
1960s groups, now leads his
own combo, and wrote the
score for *Death Wish,*
among other movies.
(Photo: Veryl Oakland)

7

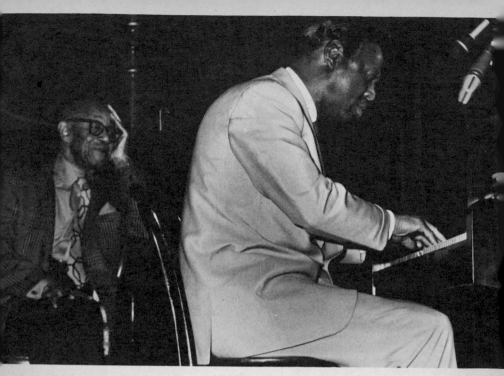

Earl "Fatha" Hines plays; **Eubie Blake** watches.
(Photo: Ed Lawless)

Freddie Hubbard, the widely imitated
trumpet star of the 1970s.

TO DAN INGMAN

My First Melody Maker Editor

But For Whom

Other Delta Books of Interest:

CELEBRATING THE DUKE
& Louis, Bessie, Billie, Bird, Carmen,
Miles, Dizzy, & Other Heroes
by Ralph J. Gleason
Foreword by Studs Terkel

ROCK FOLK
Portraits from the Rock 'n' Roll Pantheon
by Michael Lydon

THE SOUL BOOK
by Ian Hoare, Clive Anderson, Tony Cummings,
and Simon Frith

The Pleasures of Jazz

LEADING PERFORMERS ON THEIR LIVES, THEIR MUSIC,
THEIR CONTEMPORARIES

LEONARD FEATHER

Introduction by Benny Carter

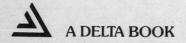 A DELTA BOOK

A Delta Book

Published by
Dell Publishing Co., Inc.
1 Dag Hammarskjold Plaza
New York, New York 10017

Reprinted by arrangement with Horizon Press Publishers, Ltd.

Delta ® TM 755118, Dell Publishing Co., Inc.

ISBN: 0-440-56946-X

Printed in the United States of America
First Delta printing—August 1977

ACKNOWLEDGEMENTS

The author acknowledges with thanks the permission of *Genesis* to reprint the two chapters on Freddie Hubbard and on twenty years of jazz; *Cavalier* for the Charles Lloyd chapter; *Melody Maker,* a member of IFC Business Press Ltd., for portions of the Mercer Ellington chapter; and the *Los Angeles Times* for the chapters which appeared there. © 1966, 1967, 1968, 1969, 1970, 1971, 1972, 1973, 1974, and 1975.

CONTENTS

LIST OF ILLUSTRATIONS

INTRODUCTION by Benny Carter

In Paris, back in 1936, a letter arrived from England from a young jazz critic and writer asking if I would be interested in coming to London for the purpose of providing arrangements for Henry Hall's BBC dance orchestra. The writer of the letter was, of course, Leonard Feather. My response was affirmative; I was eager to visit England and to meet Feather, whose work I had read and admired in the *Melody Maker* and other music publications.

So we go back a long way together!

The BBC assignment was the forerunner of many musical alliances between Leonard and myself: my first English recording dates, which he negotiated and produced; a memorable concert with an all-star British orchestra at London's Hippodrome Theatre (since my work permit restricted my activities to writing, these were the only opportunities I had to play during that first visit), and some unforgettable sessions in Holland.

My deep respect for this knowledgeable and articulate man has grown during the years and has led to a warm and special friendship which far outweighs our professional association.

It is almost impossible to enumerate in so brief a statement the diversity of Leonard Feather's talents and his many roles in the music scene. He is not only a writer of great objectivity and substance; he has produced many successful recordings from way back in the days of the 78s until the present time; he has always had an uncanny knack for recognizing and promoting new talent and was staging jazz concerts even before they became fashionable.

In recent years Leonard has broadened his horizons to include college seminars. He has given a history of jazz course at University of California at Riverside and Loyola-Marymount College in Los Angeles, as well as appearing as lecturer at dozens of campuses throughout the United States.

It may come as a surprise to the uninitiated to hear the music and lyrics of his *Evil Gal Blues* (the song that launched the career of the late Queen of the Blues, Dinah Washington), *How Blue Can You Get* (made famous by B.B. King) and *Mighty Like the Blues,* which I was first to record, during the session in Holland.

Leonard studied piano as a young man growing up in England, and continues to play whenever the opportunity presents itself. He can be heard on album he produced in Hollywood called *The Night Blooming Jazzmen,* which also features trumpeter Blue Mitchell, saxophonist Ernie Watts and organist Charles Kynard among others, playing all Feather originals.

One of his most durable songs, *Signing Off,* which he still uses for that purpose on his KBCA Radio show, was recorded by Ella Fitzgerald. And such luminaries as the late Cannonball Adderley, Phil Woods, Louis Bellson, have all cut their own renditions of Leonard's tribute to Charlie Parker, *I Remember Bird.* A particular favorite of mine is *Whisper Not,* written with saxophonist Benny Golson, of which there are several fine recorded versions.

As to Leonard's literary output, I have derived much pleasure—and information—from his *Encyclopedia of Jazz* series, *The Book of Jazz From Then Till Now, From Satchmo to Miles,* and his excursion into humor in *Laughter From the Hip,* written in collaboration with Jack Tracy. I was, therefore, flattered and delighted—if a little apprehensive—when Leonard asked me to write the introduction for this new work of his.

The Pleasures of Jazz is everything the title implies. It runs the gamut from traditionalists Barney Bigard and Red Norvo to such contemporary experimentors as Chick Corea, Herbie Hancock and Freddie Hubbard. Not only the instrumentalists but also the chanteuses (and, of course, the chanteurs) are here. There is even a definitive portrait of the Newport Years.

Though we may be familiar with some of the artists represented in this book through their lives, records and concert appearances, we often learn unknown aspects of their careers: for instance, that at the age of fifty Yusef Lateef was working diligently towards his Ph.D.; that singer Cleo Laine scored some of her greatest triumphs on the legitimate stage; and that other performers had unusual, often nonmusical backgrounds that give them unique personal dimensions.

The Mercer Ellington story will be fascinating to those not acquainted with this talented son of the Twentieth Century legend of jazz. And the historical value of John Lewis's feelings about the breakup of the then twenty-year-old Modern Jazz Quartet is unquestionable.

The chapters of this book will do much to bolster the realization that jazz, long the stepchild of the music world, has now become universally recognized as a special and unique form of American culture. Leonard Feather played no small part in helping to bring this about. He has earned from musicians and jazz lovers all over the globe an enviable reputation for his illuminating and honest appraisals.

This book, apart from its amusing anecdotes, will give the reader insights into the human qualities of the artists, often expressed in their own words. Even though I have been actively involved in the world of music for many, many years, on reading Leonard's insights into jazz and the people who make it, I found much that is interesting and enlightening throughout this book.

May you find *The Pleasures of Jazz* truly a pleasurable experience.
                                                    —Beverly Hills, California

THE PLEASURES OF JAZZ

Benny Green, the eminent British critic and musician, writing about an album by Ella Fitzgerald and discussing a blues track, advises the listener to consider "its bonhomie, its vitality, its enthusiasm, its warmth." He adds that "casting aside for the moment all the arcane considerations of phrasing and range and interpretation and style, I would say that people surged to see Ella in London for the same reason that people surge to hear her everywhere else—because she makes them feel good." Mr. Green concludes that "Jazz after all started out to be a happy music, a music of release and exultation . . . Ella's blues was not only esthetically rewarding but positively therapeutic in its remedial effects. Patrons went home from Ronnie Scott's Club after watching her in action, feeling better than when they arrived. What artist could ever hope to do more?"

There is doubtless an element of oversimplification in these comments. No observer who has studied jazz in all its ramifications will deny the validity of the ghetto blues, work songs and other early forms with their inherent burden of misery. Nor will it be contested that in recent years the politicization of music, principally along radical lines, has become a raging issue, the subject of debate, of much serious writing and of diatribe. More to the point here is that in his observations about Ella Fitzgerald, Benny Green has zeroed in on an aspect of the jazz art—of all the arts—that is too often overlooked in these critical times: much of it is designed to give pleasure to the listener. Whether this pleasure takes a luxuriantly sensual, subtly humorous or overtly comedic form, a joyous gratification of the senses is involved.

There is often a tendency to equate pleasure with frivolous amusement. The truth is, of course, that the joys of jazz, though superficial at times, more often run demonstrably deep, and that the sensations they evoke are no less profound for being agreeable.

Glancing back over the history of this music and of the creative people who have brought it to life, we find in its church origins an auspicious significance in the jubilation of gospel music; the singers sang their praises by "making a joyful noise unto the Lord"—a tradition that carried through to the days of Mahalia Jackson and Clara Ward. Later, as instrumental jazz took shape, it revealed characteristics that were to earn it a lasting identity as a music of happiness as much as of the other human emotions.

Two of the most vital contributors to jazz in its formative years, Louis Armstrong and Earl Hines, both considered themselves entertainers as well as artists. Hines to this day insists that his primary function is this form of pleasurable communication.

As one of the most serious and influential composers of the 20th century, Duke Ellington maintained an attitude toward his music and his life that often expressed itself in pleasure and humor. Even such important works as *Black, Brown & Beige* and the sacred concerts were laced with touches of mordant wit. The plunger mute sounds of Tricky Sam Nanton's trombone, the sly fun of Rex Stewart's half-valve cornet, were none the less meaningful or artistically valuable for the presence of wit. Ellington was also the author of *Monologue,* a delightful free-form poem which he took pleasure in performing at concerts.

The entire big band era resounded with cheerful overtones. That many of those who listened to the most important orchestras of the day—Lunceford, Basie, Goodman, Ellington—were sometimes caught up as much in the pleasures of jitterbugging as in listening to great soloists and arrangements did not in any way lessen the intrinsic significance of the performances.

With the passing of the swing era and the emergence of bebop, a new and enduring genre was primarily the creation of Charlie Parker—whose pleasures during his appearances took several forms: odd quotes during an improvised solo, caustic comments to an apathetic or un-comprehending audience—and of Dizzy Gillespie, whose fame as a comedian has often enhanced the undimmed grandeur of his musical contribution. Bop singing, an inherently entertaining facet of the movement, soon led to the ingenious and diverting concept of setting lyrics to bop solos, first performed by individuals, such as Eddie Jefferson and King Pleasure, and most notably by a group, Lambert, Hendricks & Ross. All these singers reflected in their work the same qualities that led Benny Green to make the insightful remarks about Ella Fitzgerald quoted above.

During the 1940s and '50s the American scene was immeasurably enriched by Norman Granz's Jazz at the Philharmonic. In the spirit of the jam session significance played no role, but friendly rivalry was a cheerful element. Nobody who heard, say, Johnny Hodges, Benny

Books

Carter and Charlie Parker in a non-competitive series of solos on the same album can fail to respond to the mutual stimulation in those reciprocally joyful performances.

Jazz, like every art form, is bound to be the subject of study of its anatomy, and its sociological and racial implications. My own awareness of this should be clear to anyone who has read my first book, *Inside Bebop,* or the *Anatomy of Improvisation* chapter in my later work, *The Book of Jazz from Then till Now.* Since then, various books, such as the indispensable *Early Jazz* by Gunther Schuller, have examined the music from the academic standpoint that is essential to complete understanding of its nature.

But after a lifetime devoted in large measure to involvement with jazz, I find on looking back that the moments I remember most fondly are not simply those that proved the most durable esthetically but also those that gave me truly ecstatic delight when I first heard them. I recalled many of those moments while writing about the men and women whose personalities as well as musical contributions and opinions on a wide range of subjects make up the essence of this book, and in a couple of instances my interest in them as fascinating human beings took precedence over my sense of their importance as performers.

I am grateful to Ben Raeburn of Horizon Press not only for his invaluable editing but also for suggesting the title, to which my immediate reaction was, appropriately, one of unalloyed pleasure; to my indomitable associate Frankie Nemko, whose enthusiasm for and understanding of the music made our collaboration a long and happy one; and, as always, to Jane Feather for her patience and proofreading, tea and empathy.   —North Hollywood, California

OVERVIEW (Twenty Years of Jazz)

It was the squarest of times and the hippest of times. (Twenty Two)

For the hip it was a time when jazz, after four decades as a cultural Cinderella, took hold to an extent none of us had thought possible.

The Newport generation, as it can be called from a twenty-year vantage point, had two vital elements in common with the Woodstock generation—its music had become an international phenomenon, enjoying unprecedented coverage, and was the newly adopted sound of the young; second, it was a fast-growing source of revenue for all the acquisitive figures at the business end of music: booking agents, record producers, and impresarios.

Quantitatively, the emergence of jazz was an accomplishment far less overwhelming than that of rock in the seventies; but by way of compensation, it enjoyed unique privileges. Official recognition was accorded by the U.S. State Department through regular *Voice of America* broadcasts and, later on, dozens of overseas goodwill junkets, with Dizzy Gillespie's orchestra picked as the first ambassadors in 1956. But most of all, it acquired during those pivotal years a degree of acceptance that transcended age, class, and race barriers. Jazz was searching desperately for a cachet, a sense of legitimacy, and at this level Newport became a most telling symbol.

Just as Norman Granz has been almost singlehandedly responsible for creating the touring jazz concert in 1944 (and with virtually no support from the media), it was George Wein, then operating two jazz clubs and giving jazz lectures in Boston, who got it all together for the American festival.

Dave Brubeck recalled: "George took us out on a tour in 1953. He was driving, and my whole quartet was in one car. He kept saying that there must be an audience outside of night clubs, where jazz could be presented in a manner that would establish it as a respected art form. That was all he talked about; he was going to do this somehow, if he could just find the backing and the location."

One of the students at Wein's Boston University jazz classes was an attractive woman named Elaine Lorillard, whose husband was the wealthy Louis P. Lorillard of the socialite Newport crowd. Wein's obsession intrigued her. The Lorillards, who had considerable clout in

the Newport community, came to play a major role in underwriting
Wein's concept of a festival of jazz. James Van Alen, president of the
Newport Casino, was gently persuaded that no harm could result from
using the center court of the casino's tennis grounds as the festival's
setting.

Underlying the event, of course, was the psychological element inherent in presenting, under the auspices and in the presence of the
socially prominent, a program of music that had never quite shaken off
its identity as the product of whorehouses. By 1954 there were in
Newport enough business, civic, and social leaders receptive to jazz to
constitute a sponsoring committee.

The operational expenses for the two-night gala, headlined in *Down
Beat* as a "Huge Summer Jazz Festival," were set at $10,000—a
small fraction of what the Rolling Stones now earn in a single concert;
yet this budget enabled Wein to hire a dozen top combos, three name
singers, and Stan Kenton. Since there was no money to fly in his band
from the West Coast, Stan was there for his name value and his services as narrator. The show was announced as "A Living History of
American Jazz."

The initiative worked. From the opening strains of *Muskrat Ramble*,
played by Eddie Condon's Dixieland combo on Saturday, July 17,
through the last thump of Gene Krupa's bass drum shortly after midnight Sunday, the crowd (a combined attendance of 13,000) was
mature and attentive.

The climax of the concert for most of us was the appearance, late
Sunday evening, of Billie Holiday. Earlier that year I had taken Lady
Day on her first (and, as it turned out, only) European tour, starring in a
package show with Buddy De Franco, Red Norvo, and others. By that
time Billie was past her peak, and some skeptics doubted that she
would be able to make much of an impression, particularly in the light
of a wild ovation that had greeted Ella Fitzgerald at the Saturday concert.

But the Lady's matchless beauty, her almost tangible sensuality, the
subtle, compelling reshaping of every lyric and melody, completely
conquered the audience.

Sexual attraction played a negligible role in the appeal of jazz;
vocally and instrumentally most of the music was devoid of erotic
overtones. Lady was an exception. So was Lee Wiley, who sang at the
opening concert. Stunningly she sang in a husky, intimate style that
had more than a little in common with the distinctive timbre of another

woman who that same night was performing in the summer theater at the far end of the casino, Tallulah Bankhead.

Tallulah is gone now; so are Condon and Krupa and Lady Day, along with two others who were in Newport over the catalytic weekend, Pee Wee Russell and Lester Young. Lee Wiley has died. But it speaks volumes for the staying power of jazzmen that of the other major names at the first festival, every one is active over twenty years after. Lennie Tristano is a teacher, Gil Melle turned to electronic music and film scores, while the rest remain as visible as ever: Dizzy Gillespie, Lee Konitz, Oscar Peterson, Milt Jackson, Horace Silver, Gerry Mulligan, George Shearing, Teddy Wilson. (Can you imagine an analogous situation at a rock show twenty years from now?)

"This is the only new thing in Newport since Henry James," said Elaine Lorillard. "This is my dream come true," George Wein told reporters. "Jazz has come of age."

Newport was the most convincing proof for the case for jazz at that time. During the same year, Dave Brubeck landed his memorable *Time* cover story (later there would be one for Thelonious Monk). Magazines that had long ignored jazz ran heavy intellectual features. Even *The Nation's Business* printed a story on Lionel Hampton. New York's hitherto sacrosanct classical radio station, WQXR, started its first-ever jazz record series. The television networks, a medium least hospitable to any music as art, dipped their corporate toes in the suddenly holy water during the middle and late Fifties with an occasional special, climaxed by a superb presentation by CBS called *The Sound of Jazz*, with Lady Day, Lester Young, Jimmy Rushing, Count Basie, Ben Webster, and Coleman Hawkins.

In fact, jazz was for a few wild years the eye of a hurricane. The mere use of the word had as much built-in commercial value in the offices of a & r men as it had pejorative meanings by the time rock had taken over. In 1954, after years of neglect, RCA announced a big push on jazz; Capitol designated Stan Kenton to enroll combos for a new *Kenton Presents* jazz schedule. Norman Granz, having recorded more material than his Clef Records catalogue could accommodate, launched a second label, Norgran Records. Every company joined the stampede. The cry was: *Find us some jazz! We don't want to be left out!* One executive, Archie Bleyer, was asked why he had gone into jazz with his Cadence Records. He replied, "The jazz market is growing by leaps and bounds. Jazz has become an important and profitable part of the music business."

But it was also, as I said in the beginning before my enthusiasm got the better of me, the squarest of times. It was a time when life could be a dream, sh'boom; when the Crew Cuts' record of that song was more representative of middle America's tastes than anything jazz could offer. The Ames Brothers, the Four Lads, the Clovers were pistol-hot. The rhythm and blues field was trundling out such trivia as LaVern Baker's *Tweedlee Dee*.

We were even conscious that rock was undergoing a metamorphosis from a euphemistic verb (which jazz also had been a half century earlier) into half of a double-barreled noun: Chuck Berry made this a *fait accompli* with a song in 1957 actually called "Rock and Roll Music." By April of 1956 the wave of the future splashed us in a *Down Beat* headline: "Teeners Riot in Massachusetts and Cause Rock and Roll Ban."

Still, the events that concerned those of us who were a happy, involved part of our own scene were the vastly increased availability of high-caliber jazz, the proliferation of cross-country tours (the Granz concept had spawned a dozen imitations), the growing attention accorded the music at the academic level (jazz credit courses were rare but increasing), and the incredible success of the medium's search for acceptance.

To the Newport generation, every profile of a jazzman in *The New Yorker*, every acknowledgment of its viability through incorporation into a movie (even such a moronic fiasco as *The Benny Goodman Story*), every new book about jazz, every appearance of Duke Ellington on a major television show, was another victory for Our Side. Respectability was the name of the game; why else did the Modern Jazz Quartet bow so stiffly, avoid smiling at all costs, and wear those swallow tail coats that led some observers to dub them the Four Undertakers?

This quest for dignity stemmed not only from the need to escape from the image of bawdy house beginnings, but also from the damage suffered during a near-epidemic of heroin addiction among prominent jazzmen throughout the preceding decade. Charlie Parker and Billie Holiday were among the first; later Miles, Getz, Anita O'Day, Mulligan and others made unwanted headlines.

In a blistering attack on the junkies and the "imbecilic cultists" who fawned on them, Oscar Peterson declared that, "If the jazz scene continues the way it is going today, I don't want to be a part of it very much longer."

Drugs at that time were only three in number. Alcohol was legal and therefore accepted, regardless of its ravages on the jazzmen who had come up in the Prohibition years. Pot, then known as tea or weed, had been commonly used by countless jazzmen from Louis Armstrong on down, at least since World War 1, but its consumption on the public side of the footlights was almost zero, except among an inside clique of fans who had grown personally close to the musicians. Heroin became the greatest scourge of the Forties and Fifties; cocaine was all but unknown in jazz circles; speed, LSD and other mind-alterers were uninvented or unheard of.

The difference in the drug situation was one of several contrasts between the Newport lifestyle and the Woodstock Weltanschauung. To set it in perspective one must go back to a period that predated both Newport and Woodstock—the era of swing. Swing music, for all its musical success, was associated in the public mind with jitterbugging. The picture of jazz as a utilitarian music for Roseland and the Savoy Ballroom faded all too slowly. Thus the triumphs of the 1950s were linked to the belated recognition of jazz as serious music for listening. If you could persuade your parents, even your music teacher, to attend a concert or festival with you, so much the better.

Rock 'n' Roll, in all its phases from Beatles to Bowie, represents an antithetical stance on the part of audience and performer alike. The parents' values were ignored. There was a return to show-biz pretentiousness; what Lennon, McCartney and others stood for, visually and viscerally, made an impression far beyond just the songs and the lyrics. Drugs became commonplace among listeners as well as performers. Fashions and modes of living were dictated by the new cult heroes; rock became a transcendent trip appealing to all the senses. It was at once more and less than a musical revolution. The claim that rock has drawn the biggest crowds in the history of music evades a central point: vast numbers of those who went to Woodstock or Watkins Glen were physically beyond earshot even of those threshold-of-pain sounds. America's youth was on hand for the happening—*being there* was an event in itself. Jazz never quite aspired to that kind of attitude. It merely asked for, and ultimately gained, attentive and sensitive ears.

Granted, comparisons are made difficult by the huge fourteen-to-twenty-four percent population growth of the past two decades, the post-World War II infants having only recently reached their majority. There are also sharp contrasts between the relative stability of the Newport youth movement and the disenchantment of a later generation from the social, racial, and political traumas of the 1960s. Nevertheless, to the extent that it was possible, Newport and the other jazz achievements of the 1950s provided a direct antecedent for Woodstock and much that it still represents.

With this in mind, I approached George Wein and a dozen other notables who were a part of that era to discover how they see the past in today's psycho-funkedelic light, to explore their attitudes towards developments since then, and their views on problems related to the generational transition.

Asked what they miss most about those days, several hinted at a loss of innocence. "I miss the camaraderie that people who are young and single seem to have," said Cannonball Adderley. "Also the commitment to music that one makes when he is fifteen to twenty years younger." George Shearing looks back in hunger for "the variety of music that used to be available. You could go to several different clubs within walking distance in one night and hear as many different kinds of jazz."

Singer Jon Hendricks, who in 1954 had begun recording with Dave Lambert but had not yet teamed up with Annie Ross, offered a politicized recollection: "Jazz during that period was America's cultural art form for *real*. John Foster Dulles may have been the Secretary of State, but Louis Armstrong was the real Ambassador! When then-Vice President Nixon went on a goodwill tour of Venezuela (to consolidate the Rockefeller holdings there) he got stoned. I don't mean high; I mean by people throwing rocks. At his head! Booking agent Dulles, ever responsive to the public will, promptly sent in his best act—Louis Armstrong. The people threw things at Louis too—roses!

"This establishes and defines the climate then as opposed to now. Then the climate was Summer. Now it's Winter. But the wise man knows that Summer always follows Winter. And night clubs, concerts, festivals, radio, television, media coverage and the overseas market all—without exception—depend on the climate. Meanwhile, those of us who play, listen to and love jazz music have got our love to keep us warm."

Shelly Manne recalled that "even back in the 52nd Street days of World War II, jazz fans were less factionalized. Nowadays, instead of liking jazz as a whole, they tend to categorize. I know from observation at my own club that free avant-garde music, bebop, and swing or traditional jazz draw entirely different audiences. That's kinda sad."

Jazz critic Dan Morgenstern (with *Metronome* in the Fifties, *Down Beat* in the Sixties) disagreed: "Twenty years ago there was still a lingering hostility between protagonists of different styles and eras. Today audiences and critics are more open-minded, less sectarian."

One of the elements missing as much as any other, it seems to me (and my observation is shared by George Wein and Dizzy Gillespie, among others), is a constant emergence of exciting new groups and locales in which to try out fresh ideas. In New York alone, there were a dozen not-so-secluded rendezvous spots where, without a dime in his pocket, the ambitious young jazzman could sit in and jam. Within a short span, a man like Gillespie could and did work with twenty-five big bands, each with a different style. Those training grounds simply do not exist today.

Also lacking today is a togetherness of the kind one found in the band bus, on the festival grounds, or even in the funky night clubs and dance halls. In 1954, blacks and whites congregated at the Savoy, at Minton's, and other Harlem rooms without fear of violence. Downtown you might find Bird at Birdland, Condon at Condon's, Carmen McRae at Basin Street, Red Norvo at the Embers, Marian McPartland at the Hickory House, Red Allen at the Metropole. Not one of these rooms has survived, and although there are counterparts of a sort today, the atmosphere is not comparable.

Even a room like Birdland, with its many faults, had an ambiance that is gone forever. But as Dan Morgenstern has pointed out, that was part of a social phenomenon that transcended the music. Echoes of it may linger in a few spots where the audience is realy mixed and mainly over thirty years old.

While the locations may be missed, none of the musicians questioned had any nostalgia for one-night stands. Dave Brubeck has commented that the endless cross-country car ride, the buses, the freeways and tolls and turnpikes, contributed nothing except an ennui that today's generally more settled musicians are happily rid of.

Of course, one can argue that what we believe we miss about the mid-1950s is not the creativity but rather the popular success that jazz was enjoying. This point was raised by Philippe Carles, editor of France's *Jazz Magazine*. Averring that music in the show business market rarely caters to the exigencies of the artists, he commented: "In France in the late fifties Sidney Bechet, Art Blakey's Jazz Messengers and the Modern Jazz Quartet sold well; but where could the jazz student listen to such truly great innovators as Ornette Coleman and Cecil Taylor? So I miss nothing about that period.''

Though there is general agreement that jazz was widely disseminated in those salad days, opinions differ with regard to specific media. Drummer-composer Louie Bellson, a combo leader in the Fifties who nowadays fronts his own big band, lamented that ''the nightclub is almost gone now. Concerts and festivals are the only salvation.'' Cannonball Adderley added, ''the nightclub is de-emphasized and seems to be phasing out.'' George Shearing and several others agreed.

Wein and Morgenstern saw it differently, saying there were now at least as many jazz clubs as there were in the Fifties—perhaps more—particularly in New York. The contradiction was clarified by Joe Newman, the ex-Basie trumpeter who doubled as president of Jazz Interactions, a nonprofit organization that promotes a variety of jazz events. ''Sure, we may have fifty rooms in New York,'' said Newman, ''but most of them scarcely have the room or the bread for a trio or duo. In the early years we not only had clubs that could house a big band but also the hotel rooms—the Lincoln, Commodore, New Yorker, Statler, Waldorf—where you could listen and dance to the great orchestras.'' Clark Terry, a key figure in the Ellington brass section through the Fifties and an intensely busy man nowadays at campus concerts and workshops, amplified the point: ''Dancing has become less popular; we have fewer outlets in the dance halls and hardly any club owners willing to gamble on big bands—and, consequently, fewer big bands.''

Part of the nightclub and dance hall slack was taken up for a time by the concert tours and festivals that proliferated with all too deliberate speed in the late fifties. Newport led to such short-lived projects as Wein's French Lick, Indiana Jazz Festival; of these early ventures only Monterey, launched by Jimmy Lyons in 1958, has survived. The jazz package tour also became a victim of overcrowding. In 1954 Stan Kenton was able to take out two shows under his ''Festival of Modern Jazz'' banner; one with Art Tatum and others, the second with Dizzy, Bird, Erroll Garner, et al.

''Jazz For Moderns,'' which I emceed, went out in 1958 and '59 with Brubeck's Quartet, Maynard Ferguson's band, Sonny Rollins' Trio and Lambert, Hendricks & Ross. Our own chartered plane took us to such unlikely venues as Tulsa, Okla., Blacksburg, Va., and Cedar

Falls, Iowa. Logistics, economics, and simple lack of demand would make this unthinkable today.

The aspiring jazz musician in the seventies is left to make it very much on his own. When Norman Granz was flourishing, he elevated the stature of musicians in ways that are now taken for granted. As Gillespie and others who worked for him recall, he pioneered in insisting on first-class accommodation and treatment. Desegregation, not easily accomplished then, was written into every Granz contract. In addition, as Dizzy observed: "The music was a challenge, a ball, because Norman got the best cats all the time. That informal jam session-concert spirit isn't around any more."

Though he gave up his U.S. concert tours in 1957, Granz continued to function actively in Europe. Even at this late date, jazz suffers from the prophet-without-domestic-honor syndrome. Buddy De Franco, the eminent clarinetist (he tied with Benny Goodman for first place in the 1954 *Down Beat* critics' poll), returned to jazz after eight years as front man for the Glenn Miller ghost band—a job he took because jazz had failed to earn him a living. But the overseas market remained healthy for him; it was during his tours of Japan that he received the greatest number of requests to suspend the Miller mood and blow a few jazz tunes. Clark Terry and many others have confirmed that the exposure given jazz on European television and in Japan pointed up the more mature appreciation of this American genre among overseas audiences.

As Jon Hendricks remarked, everything moves in cycles: "Caught in the media-motivated social world, people move away from jazz and claim it's dying, only to return to it and tell us it's coming back. Like the sun, jazz never moves; everything revolves around it. Just as when part of the earth turns away from the sun, people say it's night, so it is with jazz but it can no more die than the sun, it can no more be evaluated by man than the sun. In the end one can only bask in the warmth of both, and be thankful for one's awareness of them."

From his base in Milan, Arrigo Polillo, editor of *Musica Jazz*, took a gloomier view. "In Italy a Led Zeppelin album will outsell Duke Ellington at least fifty to one. The incredible impact of rock on the juvenile audience is largely responsible for the downfall of jazz. The ears of the youngsters are adjusted to electronic sounds; jazz to them seems too jaded, and too difficult. There is no comparison between the coverage of jazz and of rock by the press, radio and TV; jazz is considered by the mass media operators to be a music for a small elite, and, worse, for an outmoded clique."

Whatever the problems faced at home or abroad, the academic community is helping to resolve them. Jazz in its early stages was based more on the msuicians' innate feeling than on formal schooling. Today, distinguished jazz musicians by the score are at Yale, Princeton, Rutgers; at universities, schools, and colleges clear across the country to give courses in jazz and black history. Joe Newman, as part of his work with Jazz Interactions, has been deeply involved with this movement, and never merely as an entertainer. The classes, clinics, and workshops of the past decade established jazz education as a vital force for progress in an area that had long seemed impregnable.

There are now 30,000 stage bands at high schools, most of them jazz oriented. "I've been helping young people master their craft," Clark Terry told me, "and I find that, thanks to these opportunities, jazz has progressed tremendously." This conclusion would seem irrefutable, but Dan Morgenstern dissents. "Sure, there are plenty of well-equipped kids coming out of Berklee College and the rest; but there has been no comparable artistic improvement. I'm not a believer in progress in the arts. Change, yes. Progress, no. Jazz was once a folk art, and there was no need for progress there, so I'm against the whole concept. I see no real ground having been broken since the advent of Ornette Coleman in the late Fifties. John Coltrane's development continued into the Sixties, but he lost me somewhere in there. I see 'progress' only in the sphere of appreciation; young people today are open to every sound from Bessie Smith to Ornette."

With the Woodstock yearlings learning about jazz at school while being indoctrinated into rock via top-40 radio, it might be assumed that a jazz-rock merger would be the inevitable result. Opinions on this point differed heatedly. George Wein's was the strongest negative response: "A merger is not only *not* inevitable, but whatever amalgamation there has been will disappear completely soon. The rock mode is far too limited for the real artistry of a true jazzman." Cannonball Adderley and Dan Morgenstern agreed. The latter's comment: "Rock is almost exclusively a pop music, an entertainment music. Cross currents have been part of the picture, but the most advanced rock listeners (that is, those who dig the music, not the social-sexual aspects that dominate it) will, given the exposure, probably defect to jazz."

Clark Terry replied: "It's true that one will rub off on the other, but jazz as a separate entity will survive." Gillespie said: "A merger ain't no big thing, since rock is just an offshoot of jazz. When I play rock, I'm still playing Dizzy Gillespie. If I'm in Spain and want to play flamenco music, I'll do it in my style." Shelly Manne concurred: "Rock stole from r & b, which jazz also stemmed from, so the merger is really a reunion."

Bellson felt the merger was here, and that many of the valid components of rock will remain permanently. Philippe Carles declared: "The merger is with us, due to fashion's pressure, which means economic power—inevitable in a capitalistic system." De Franco said: "It's unavoidable, but it will cause erosion and decay of high musical standards."

According to Jon Hendricks, "merger is a very flattering term. From jazz rock came, and to jazz it shall return."

But these comments have missed a crucial point. It is entirely possible that rock will absorb jazz on some levels, will coexist with it on others, and in certain instances, jazz will remain totally untouched by the impact of the Woodstock generation. A parallel can be seen at any session of a Dixieland Jazz Society. At the meetings of such organizations, which continue to flourish in many urban centers neither the players nor the listeners seem to have caught on to the fact that there have been any new developments since 1930! The worlds of music never have been monolithic; they will continue to operate on diverse plateaus no matter how violent the revolutions of today or tomorrow.

An aspect of the change in jazz that has been of great concern to this writer, as it has to students and musicians everywhere, is the racial polarization most observers feel has taken place. For many who felt the good interracial vibes of the Newport years, the music was a virtual symbol of rapprochement. Today, doubtless as a consequence of the social upheavals during the turbulent 1960s, a schism appears to have emerged.

A minority of those answering my questions felt that racism is less a factor roday. "It is certainly less prevalent among musicians than in society," said Cannonball Adderley, "and less influenced by social problems than during the Fifties."

It is arguable that many musicians utilize their blackness as a viable commercial commodity, but that their only real concern is the ability of their colleagues to play. This is the view—perhaps wishful, but he was not alone in expressing it—of George Wein. The point was also made by Dizzy Gillespie that at one time Benny Goodman was the only man in the field who had put integration into public practice, whereas today the mixed band is a rule rather than an exception.

The problem, however, goes much beyond such surface achievements. More and more in recent years musicians and a number of critics (including some whites) have espoused the theory that true jazz can only be created by blacks. Joe Newman and others have attributed this polarization to the evident fact that, as musicians in search of their roots, blacks *know* the music had begun with them; but their role had been played down for so long that this injustice could only be alleviated by playing it up just as heavily.

Racial issues aside, there remains the problem of whether today's youth can relate to jazz as readily as to rock, provided they are given an extensive opportunity to hear it.

Of those with whom I discussed this issue, only George Wein sounded skeptical: "Rock is a social music. Jazz can be social only if it involves dancing. The intellectual and emotional demands necessary for full appreciation of jazz will probably keep today's youth, or the youth of any day, from relating to it en masse." Yet Wein's own experience in bringing Newport to New York and expanding its scope during the last few years surely refutes his own theory.

The many difficulties encountered during the long, roller-coaster Newport-to-Woodstock detour were succinctly summarized by Joe Newman:

"The revolution we've been going through in the young people's rebellion against established ideas has estranged them from their parents; but the parents, out of desperation, have tried to join them, find a common ground.

"That should give us an advantage. There is a contrast between today's situation and that of the World War II years, which provided the background for so much of the growth of modern jazz. During the old war, there wasn't a family that wanted to keep their son out on moral grounds, whereas during the Vietnam years, parents who didn't want their children mixed up in it helped them avoid fighting in a conflict that had no meaning to this country. So you had rebellious young people with their own beliefs, their rejection of anyone and anything they felt symbolized outdated attitudes; and along with it, their own music."

It is indeed arguable that factors such as these governed an entire lifestyle during the chaotic Vietnam years. Newman added optimistically that "When we get Vietnam and Watergate completely behind us, we're going to be a different people, and I think by then jazz will really be swinging high again."

In some respects, the analogy has begun to be proven, and the predicted resurgence is on its way, triggered in large measure by the fortunate accident of Newport's enforced move from its home base to the Manhattan area. The stoned fools on the hill who broke through fences, stormed the Newport arena, and wrecked the stage in 1971 were not jazz fans but footloose trippers in search of some wild action. They were a blessing in disguise: the following summer found the festival enlarged to eight days and dozens of concerts spread all over the New York metropolitan area. Media coverage was without precedent; Dick Cavett devoted an entire program to participants in the events, all three newspapers ran features (the *Times* had as many as six reports in a single issue); few national magazines failed to pay homage to Newport's invasion of the big city.

Nor was this explosion lost on the businessmen who had long since shrugged off jazz as a corpse. Clubs around town switched to a jazz policy; record companies have reissued, in ever-growing quantities, jazz material that had lain dormant in their vaults for years.

Of course, jazz remains a music of minority appeal as it has always been. Even at the peak of the swing era, the Guy Lombardos and Kate Smiths were for the most part outselling Benny Goodman and Artie Shaw. For a brief moment in 1954, Columbia Records let it be known that Dave Brubeck was growing more on LPs than Liberace; but that was a rare exception. Despite the upsurge in jazz clubs, the great advances at the academic level, the flood of records, an inescapable fact holds true; jazz is responsible for about two percent of all LP sales while rock accounts for approximately sixty-six percent. (On the other hand, the potential life for a jazz release is incomparably longer.)

Behind these paradoxes lies another one, somewhat subtler, and pointed out to me in a conversation with Dave Brubeck. After Benny Goodman had played at Ravinia, it was decided never again to present jazz there because of the disruption he had caused. In fact, before a concert Brubeck played there some years later, he was taken downtown, shown the credo of the park, and forced to promise that he would "quit playing if the audience started jitterbugging in the aisles!"

What has happened since then, of course, is that rock has taken some of the brunt, some of the punishment formerly meted out to jazz, while the latter is now considered practically Establishment. There is a curious irony here. The music that promoters were once afraid to bring into Carnegie Hall and other places where it is now almost an everyday occurrence has become a sort of classic music and no longer a risk. Recordings of the music of Scott Joplin and Jelly Roll Morton have been released on the Red Seal, Masterworks, and other classical labels. It can only be a matter of moments before Duke Ellington and others once assigned to the race lists for the ghetto will be similarly elevated to classical stature.

The point of all this is an axiom that has applied to all the arts through the centuries: yesterday's outrage is today's norm. One can only hope that this will not discourage the progeny of Woodstock from joining minds and hands with the men and women—some of them graying and paunchy now, but unflagging in their enthusiasm—who represent the Newport generation.

HAPPENINGS

schoologhard bops.

Freddie Hubbard

There was a strange turn of events at the 1972 Newport Jazz Festival in New York. To show his independence on the Fourth of July, Miles Davis refused to show up.

Unfazed, producer George Wein substituted Freddie Hubbard for the two Carnegie Hall gigs. Only sixty refunds were requested, and these tickets were quickly resold to Hubbard enthusiasts. When Wein told the audience, "Mr. Davis regrets he's unable to blow today," the announcement that Hubbard would replace him drew applause. The performances by the young trumpeter's quintet brought a standing ovation at both houses.

Who is Frederick DeWayne Hubbard? "One of the world's greatest trumpet players," to quote Freddie Hubbard. He made the claim in 1970 as a panelist appearing on the Dick Cavett show during which he complained about the short shrift accorded jazz and black musicians on television.

Today Hubbard shows signs of the ability to pick up the pieces dropped by Davis. The latter, seemingly obsessed by the conviction that rock is where it's at, has left a substantial proportion of his former followers searching for a fearless new leader. In Hubbard they have found a man whose roots are deep and widespread, whose training (formally at Jordan Conservatory and informally with Art Blakey in the school of hard bops) equipped him for any contingency. What other trumpeter-fluegelhornist-composer, after blending effortlessly into the free-jazz abstractions of Ornette Coleman and taping a couple of dates with John Coltrane, could then go through some r & b changes, and finally hit the aesthetic-commercial jackpot in a series of records with woodwinds and strings, playing everything from the McCartneys' *Uncle Albert/Admiral Halsey* to a composition written eleven years before he was born, Bix Beiderbecke's *In A Mist*? A long question, a short answer: only the cat known to his friends as Hub Cap.

A long, painful maturation took Hubbard from his eclectic beginnings as an admirer of Dizzy Gillespie, Clifford Brown, and Miles Davis to his present eminence.

Hubbard: "There were six of us—three boys, three girls. I was the baby, an Aries, April 7, 1938. With everybody growing up and leaving, it put a lot of responsibility on me. My father and mother broke up when I was nine. I moved from house to house with my mother because rent money was always short. I remember seeing my father come home with his arm damn near burned off. He worked in the steel mill until the pressures were more than he could take. He'd drink all the time. I loved my parents dearly; they're both dead now.

"Having a white grandfather on my father's side was very confusing. He had blue eyes and blond hair, and his own church. He'd sit all day reading the Bible. Beautiful. His wife was very dark complected. They'd moved to Indianapolis from the South. My mother had some Indian in her. Indian people have their own way of thinking about things. She never wanted to go to the doctor; she felt she could heal herself through prayers. Being so religious, she disapproved of jazz— you know, I was playing the devil's music. I was originally into the Flamingoes and all those singing groups, then my brother Earmon, Jr. turned me on to jazz. Every day I'd wake up and he'd have Charlie Parker on. Finally my mother let me play but she didn't want me to make a career out of it.

"Indianapolis was always a very conservative city, but oddly enough, ever since 1933, they'd been busing. So I was one of fifty blacks in a school of four thousand five hundred. I felt I was getting an educational advantage, but the faculty wasn't ready for integration. My history teacher was a former KKK member. It was weird, thinking you'd know an answer and holding up your hand, and a teacher would go right past me and ask someone else, a white kid. But I wasn't bitter; I just felt they didn't understand me and I didn't understand them. I was one of the better students, and I was never one of those ruffian types, but living in the ghetto you had to run with teenaged gangs or they'd pick on you and make you a scapegoat. So I ran with some pretty rough company. You didn't dare cry; you had to fight.

"I had one white friend in the integrated school, and I used to go into his neighborhood just to see how white people lived. And I started digging chicks. We'd meet on railroad trestles, in alleys, in cars, and kiss. I'll never forget when this one teacher caught me and this chick kissing in the cloakroom. They took us before the dean, and the girl's parents took her out of school. Chicks used to come and pick me up . . . can you imagine them roaring into the ghetto in their big fine cars on a hot summer day, and everybody's sitting on the porch, saying what is *this?*

"I can go back into the ghetto now and understand where those people are coming from. My whole early life was a constant hassle. In this attic where we lived, I'd heat up some water, pour it into a tub and sit beside a cold stove. Out of the attic window I might see Wes Montgomery in the street washing milk trucks. I saw him struggling, but I never looked at life then as being a struggle; I just figured, make the best you can of it."

L.F.: "How did you escape from that environment to a point where you could get into music seriously?"

F.H.: "A black teacher named James Compton got me off the street. He said "Try music. You seem to have talent." It it hadn't been for him, by now I'd probably be a junkie, or dead. Pretty soon I was winning all-city and all-state contests, playing mellophone. Then I was offered a scholarship at Central State College, on French Horn. I couldn't take it, though, because my general grades weren't good enough, so instead I went to Jordan Conservatory. By now I was also playing trumpet, studying harmony and counterpoint. When I was about to join the conservatory, I dated a chick whose father was a bank president. One night after I'd dropped her off at her suburban home, a cop stopped me and said 'You're under arrest.' I spent two and a half days in jail for suspicion of burglary. They dismissed the charge, of course; it was just racist hassling. So before I left Indianapolis I became very bitter."

L.F.: "Did you get to know any white musicians? Was there any exchange of ideas between the races?"

F.H.: "Yes, I knew John Bunch—he was Tony Bennett's musical director—and Conte Candoli, who was from Mishawaka, was in town sometimes and I'd check him out. We had a white pianist in a combo we formed to play at a local black club. We called ourselves the Jazz Contemporaries. Wes Montgomery heard me, and I got to play some gigs with him and made my first album, *The Montgomery Brothers Plus Five Others*."

[Reviewing this album, Down Beat observed: "Hubbard, 19, has some technical difficulties, including a struggle to master matters of intonation, and is less effective because of them.'' The Montgomery Brothers, the critic concluded, would have been better off just making an album of their own.]

Hubbard was barely out of his teens when a friend told him he was moving to New York and added: ''You can live with me until you get on your feet.'' Since Wes Montgomery had been urging Freddie to make the move, he took up the offer.

F.H.: ''This guy lived in the Bronx. The city frightened me so much that for a month I refused to come out of the house. I looked out the window and saw people fighting and robbing and cutting each other. I began to think, well, Indianapolis wasn't all that bad.

''During the second month I started going to jam sessions at Count Basie's club. Nobody asked me to play; finally one night I just ran up there with my trumpet and began to blow. Suddenly I looked up and saw Donald Byrd watching me. We looked just like brothers, and I kinda sounded like him, too; so I started getting some work just because people identified me with Donald. It was weird.

[New York offered a stabbing disillusionment to young Hubbard, who sought out his childhood idols, expecting them to be riding around in big cars, with homes and business operations to match, but found a starkly different picture.]

F.H.: ''I didn't drink, smoke, curse—a real country boy, you dig? And everybody I met in New York was strung out on drugs. I ended up lending money to guys who'd been my heroes, and even hiring them for gigs. I said to myself, my God, I never want to fall into that trap; so this disillusionment gave me the determination to do things right.

''I moved out from the Bronx and shared a room with two other musicians in Harlem, around the corner from the Apollo. There was three of us sleeping in a bed, and it wasn't even king size! I lived that way for a ycar and a half. I was clean, though, always kept myself looking nice. I could have become a successful pimp; prostitutes just used to beg me.

''One day I was at a jam session and this young lady was in the audience. She told me she was a nurse, and if I had no place to stay I could move in with her. So I stayed with her. She was thirty-nine and I was twenty. She had a nice place in Brooklyn, and she dug my talent. She said, 'You just practice until you get your thing together, then you can go do what you want.' It was a beautiful relationship. We rehearsed in her basement garage; I got together with Wayne Shorter and Pete La Roca and we organized a group. Soon I was making $125 a week in a Brooklyn club. While I was there I had a chance to meet Sonny Rollins and Philly Joe Jones, and later worked in their combos.''

L.F.: "Is there any truth to the legend about Miles Davis sitting in front of you at Birdland, looking up disdainfully?"

F.H.: "Yes, I was working there with Philly Joe, and I had my eyes closed, as I often do during a solo. I opened my eyes and there was Miles, and it scared me to death. I had tried for months to summon up the courage to speak to him, and he never said a word to me. So everyone asked him did he like the way I played, and over the next couple of years he said things about me that were pretty cool, even though I didn't really have it together then.''

Some observers might disagree. With the release of Hubbard's first album as a leader, auspiciously titled *Open Sesame*, every critic from Leroi Jones to Nat Hentoff was spanning the adverb-adjective spectrum: cleanly articulated, strongly assertive, tonally original, maturely imaginative. By way of confirmation, in 1960 he was hired to tour with J.J. Johnson, the poll-winning trombonist, and the following year was himself a *Down Beat* poll winner as a new star. When the Johnson group disbanded, Hubbard took time out for a new romance.

F.H.:"Brenda was a fantastically beautiful lady. She was in the black bourgeois 400 set in Brooklyn, and luckily her social group was into jazz. We decided to get married, and things got off to a strange start; we broke up on our honeymoon. I was involved in the summer school of jazz at Lenox, Massachusetts and those cats wouldn't let me have a good honeymoon, they were always knocking on my door. 'Freddie, what's happening?' They wanted me to hang out. So I sent her home.''

After the Johnson job, Hub Cap's career was in limbo. For a year his wife, a keypunch operator, took care of most of the bills, a dereliction on Hubbard's part, of which he now observes: "I should have shown my independence and taken a day job.''

A chance for big band experience opened up in the brass section of Quincy Jones's band. There was even a trip to Europe with Jones. "I was like a babe in the woods with all those older guys. They used to call me Juniflip.'' But the work still was not steady enough to assure him of security.

F.H.: "I didn't really start a permanent job until I went with Art Blakey's Jazz Messengers. Soon afterward, I was making a whole bunch of albums, composing a lot of music for records, had a publishing deal set up, and there was enough money coming in so we moved out of Brenda's mother's house and got our own place in Brooklyn.

Seven years ago, my son Duane was born. He was the only child and that was one of the main reasons my marriage was so stormy. I always wanted a big family."

L.F.: How did you happen to begin flirting with the avant garde and free jazz movement?

F.H.: "I've always been an inquisitive person; I want to know what's going on socially, politically, musically. I mean, I loved bebop—no matter how weird a guy might play, you could put your finger on it and analyze it—but John Coltrane was something else. I spent a lot of time going over to his house, asking how he got through those chord progressions. And of course I heard Ornette's music, which didn't have *any* changes; this kinda confused me, but it sounded awful hip. I could always play what they considered avant garde—that was easy; you just played. But Ornette Coleman showed me that in fact there was a lot of thought behind it. When I made that *Free Jazz* album with him, it took me about a year after it came out before I realized what was happening on it. The music was so odd, so foreign sounding. Basically, though, I still like melodies. I like romantic-sounding pieces. I dig hard-driving stuff, and I enjoy playing a soft bossa nova."

L.F.: "The Blakey experience was your longest-lasting. Did those two and a half years represent an important evolutionary period?"

F.H.: "He was a father figure. Art thrives on youth surrounding him and I admired his strength of character. He used to do things nobody else could have done without winding up in jail, and he'd always land on his feet. With Art, I had a chance to tour Japan twice, see all of Europe, talk on the mike, play and write anything I wanted to. In terms of getting my name out there, he was more helpful than any other leader." [After leaving Blakey and fronting his own group for a while, Hubbard was invited to Austria where Friedrich Gulda, the Beethoven expert doubling as jazz composer-pianist, was assembling an all-star band for an album.]

F.H.: "Gulda invited me and J.J. Johnson and Mel Lewis to join what they called the Eurojazz Orchestra. We rehearsed up in the Alps, and a lot of the people there had never seen a black cat before. At that time too, I was beginning to become bitter about the race thing; I could see how white people exploit black people in America. So I was in a strange bag; but Gulda was a pretty nice, intelligent guy, and we got along. He's an accomplished pianist, but his attempts to bring the classical and jazz things together, to my ears, didn't work. I was very displeased with that recording.

I was back in Europe soon after with Max Roach. By this time the pressures in me were growing to the bursting point, and one night they exploded. We'd had a five-hour plane ride to Austria, then a four-hour bus ride to the Alps, and no sooner do we get there than some cat is shouting 'All right, you ready to hit?' I'd had a few drinks and I was out there—mad and drunk. All of a sudden I started crying and thinking about the changes these people were taking me through. So I made a speech onstage. I said, 'You white, pasty-faced jive mother-fuckers, kiss my black ass!' And I turned around and put my ass out. Max cut the tune short and took me offstage. People banged on the dressing room like they were gonna lynch me. Then two huge policemen walked in and grabbed me and Jimmy Spaulding, the saxophonist who happened to be with me, hauled us off to jail, hit me in the jaw and took my ring and watch.

''Late that night Spaulding kept knocking on the cell door, and they moved us down into the dungeon. There were lice everywhere, and cats spitting all over the floor. That's the only time I ever slept standing up. Next morning we were accused of disturbing the peace. The police chief said why bring that problem here? We don't have that problem. I said we got that problem everywhere.''

L.F.: ''Did they drop the charge?''

F.H.: ''Yeah, but I never got my ring or watch back. Still, what the cat said kinda cooled me out, and I look at people different now. I see them as victims of ignorance, because they don't want to know about black people. And the older I get, the more I realize there's a few white people really trying to get together with blacks. Not too many, though, and no matter how tight you get, when it comes down to the nitty gritty they have a misconception of what it means to be black, of what blackness is all about.''

L.F.: ''While you were discovering all this, didn't you have a temptation to find your release through drugs?''

F.H.: ''Well, I once read a book by Timothy Leary and took a trip. In fact, I tried it about three times. That stuff has its good and bad points;

each individual's metabolism has a lot to do with it. In my case, it helped open up my mind. Before I experimented with it I was kinda shy, but after taking it, I said to myself, 'You are somebody. You're Freddie Hubbard.' Before that time, I had always wanted to be outgoing, but would keep everything locked in. Since then, I've been more confident in myself.''

[Mike Levy, Hubbard's manager for the past two years, says: "Despite all the money Freddie's making now, there's an underlying insecurity. He hasn't learned how to deal with life the way he deals with his performances. On the bandstand he's a true pro; offstage he's still going through a lot of inner turmoil."]

L.F.: "Don't you feel after all the activities of the past few years, what the media have done and what black organizations have accomplished, that the lines of communication are a little easier?''

F.H.: "On some levels. For instance, a lot of black cats have married into white families; some have been accepted, and this has brought more closeness. But on the business level it's something else. You might go to a record company with a good qualified lawyer, and you find it's hard for them to be really truthful and negotiate. Most guys have to go out and get a white lawyer, maybe a young Jewish lawyer who knows the business, because I guess their language is the same. Even though you have black cats who have been to the best universities and know the business, they just won't let them in. Television is the quickest way to get to people and the toughest medium for black musicians to crack open. I play more television when I'm in Europe than I ever get to do at home. I was in a documentary series years ago called *Look Up and Live,* but as far as the major network programs, ain't nothing happening. I had a guy call up the *Tonight* show, and they said as long as Doc Severinsen is here, you'll never get a spot. Now I don't think Doc himself would say that, but it's the people in control who don't want to see this kind of thing happening. A white guy as good as me would have gotten on the show. I don't see why I wouldn't qualify; you know. I'm a nice looking cat, and I can rap. So these kind of things discourage black artists.''

[According to Mike Levy, "We have a lot of things in the fire for Freddie, but he's impatient. Instead of rushing into TV, we want to promote him carefully through records, then build him as a personality, create an image important enough so he won't be limited to a single number just before the show goes off the air."]

F.H.: "As for records, I couldn't even get in to see Bob Thiele at Impulse Records or Creed Taylor at CTI until I had gotten my name together. Today I know a lot more about managing my own affairs, and my message to the young black people is to learn something about the business end of things, so you can avoid that period of starving to death and compromising your music."

L.F.: "You seem to have been one of the lucky ones who didn't have to sell out, while so many others have turned left and lost their ideals."

F.H.: "Well, it's very difficult to stay out of rock and make a living. Look at Donald Byrd. Here's a guy with a Ph.D. in music, studied black history and teaches at Howard U., yet he went into playing a kind of music that a couple of years ago he wouldn't have dreamed of doing. The kids are tuned into that stuff, and unless the media agree to donate time to our kind of music—well, in order to survive in this system, we have to play music that the masses can relate to.

"Miles is another instance. After he went into that electronic rock bag, everybody started sounding like Miles, trying to play weird. That's why I'm attempting to stick to something kinda grass roots, keep my feet on the ground; because with everybody using that fender rhodes piano and stuff, they'll all sound alike. I'm not putting him down; Miles is a beautiful cat and I love him, but he's always been a spoiled kid, and he's gone off in a strange direction. Now that I'm getting my shit together, Miles is gonna have to change. As far out as he's gone now, it sounds like a bunch of noise. Not so long ago a lot of young trumpeters were following Miles; now they're trying to play what I'm playing. They hear me constantly searching for new ideas, but keeping enough musicality in there so people can understand where it's at."

L.F.: "Wasn't there one occasion when you did sell out?"

F.H.: "From 1966-70 I was with Atlantic Records, and at one point I was convinced I could do something to really get to the public. All of a sudden I switched from hard-core jazz to rock, with rock cats, and they smothered me. The LP was called *Soul Experiment*, and it didn't come off because I never had the feeling for that kind of thing. I'm not gonna make that mistake again, believe me.

"After Atlantic I switched to CTI, Creed Taylor's company. What I like about him, he's able to see how a real fusion can be made without sacrificing the music. He knows where people's heads are at, what tunes will click. Every album I've had with him has been on the charts.''

The pace has quickened for Freddie Hubbard. He has toured Japan and the United States with his own group and with Nancy Wilson, has made as much as $4,000 a night for a concert. By 1972 New York no longer held the lure that had stimulated him a decade earlier; his marriage was headed for the divorce court and Hubbard headed West. Living in a North Hollywood apartment, just a tone's blow from Donte's, he can be seen sitting outside the club in his brand new gold-on-gold $18,000 Mercedes, dressed in blue and white plaid slacks, white shirt, blue vest and red bowtie. At his side is a pretty, quiet-spoken black girl who, he says, motivated him to move to California, and is straightening out his mind.

L.F.: "What other reasons did you have for leaving New York?''
F.H.: "It's beautiful out here, the pace is much easier, there's lots of space, plus when I go to bed at night I can sleep without somebody calling up at 4 a.m. saying let's hang out. I remember Quincy telling me, 'Come on, man, get out of those garbage cans.'

"The recording companies are moving out here. Also, I'll have an opportunity to do film writing, maybe even get an acting job.''
L.F.: "Does acting appeal to you?''
F.H.: "Why not? Most black people have been acting all their lives anyway. It brings out the inner self, and being an entertainer, I can see how it would help. A lot of the public has been turned off, seeing cats on the bandstand so totally involved in what they're doing that they forget about the people. You got to have some kind of charisma.''
L.F.: "Can you foresee other avenues for yourself aside from playing? How serious are you about getting into the business end of music?''
F.H.: "I want to have my own recording company and help young guys who want to play the type of music I've built my own career on. I want to help make it last, because the way this rock 'n' roll has been promoted, there's a danger I might see my music die. I'd like to do concerts with large orchestras; that's always been my dream. I get my greatest kicks in front of a big orchestra with strings, with trumpets blaring. I haven't yet appeared with any symphony, but I'm still hoping. I don't want to get into studio work; it's too confining. A movie once in a while, okay. My first was *The Pawnbroker* for Quincy, then *Blowup*, with Herbie Hancock doing the score. I did a black film, *The Bus Is Coming*, and a science fiction film. Also *Shaft's*

Big Score, and I was really bugged that I got no credit for that, because I soloed all the way through.

"It's taken a while, but all the pieces are finally coming together. I've had a lot of young cats come around and ask me how can they make it playing this kind of music? I tell them I had to hang around with the right cats, read their music, rehearse, practice a lot, play different kinds of music I didn't want to play, commercials and all that shit, but everything helped develop me into what I am today."

Where, in fact, does Freddie Hubbard stand today? At the aesthetic level, he and his music are self-explanatory. From the inner personal standpoint, it might have been said that after spending the past couple of years exploring the light at the end of the tunnel, he has finally emerged.

From the Indianapolis youth who grew up resentful and quarrelsome, he is developing into a more complete human being: still race-proud but no longer a hater, still brash but less arrogant; still a musical giant and leader of men, but beyond the stage where sonic anarchy is loosely equated with the sound of freedom.

While jazz rides out this decade of its existence as an established and viable art form, we can point to Freddie Hubbard as the most complete representative of the values that will keep it alive.

Herbie Hancock

Herbie Hancock, whose bag was once jazz, currently is the hottest new instrumentalist-leader in America, with a quintet that defies categorical definition.

His album, *Head Hunters* has racked up, at last count, a 378,000 total—more, he adds with pride, than had been sold during a comparable period in 1970 of the best-selling *Bitches Brew* by his ex-boss Miles Davis. At presstime it was number 10 on a major trade paper pop chart.

FEATHER: How can somebody like yourself, who would not normally expect it, get to be number 13 on the pop charts? How do you explain it?

HANCOCK: The only thing I can think is this music is more accessible to the general public than any music I've done in the past. However, that's not what makes it number 13 on the charts. I think that *Chameleon* and *Watermelon Man* are what's selling the album. The arrangement in *Watermelon Man* is kinda catchy, and this attracts a lot of people. And I think on *Chameleon* the bass line and the rhythm that's in the melody are getting to people.

L.F.:*Sly* I thought had a very attractive theme. Why is it called *Sly*? Is it dedicated to Sly Stone?

H.H.: Originally I was trying to write a Sly Stone type bass line. That was a beginning. We used to play it much slower when we were first developing the song, then when we laid all the other parts on top and the tempo wound up getting much faster, then the relationship to Sly Stone was obscure. But that was the inspiration for the title. In some of the things we play now you can hear a little bit of Sly Stone. I've dug him for a very long time, but I've had a difficult time figuring out how he does what he does, and being able to capture some of his uses of rhythm. It's only recently I've been able to feel like I'm getting close to it.

L.F.: Wouldn't you say that whay you're doing now in some ways represents a retrogression?

H.H.: That's one way to look at it. It's a simpler thing, certainly. I would say that the intellectualization of music doesn't necessarily make it better, and when one talks about the voicings of horns, for instance, in a somewhat more complex manner than I'm approaching now, that doesn't really make it better. That's a matter of personal taste. It has nothing to do with the value of the music. One reason I did this album was one day I was chanting, right after the break-up of the other band, and I was trying to decide what music I wanted to do. [Hancock, who some time back became a member of the Nichiren Buddhist sect, recalls that the impetus for his change of direction came to him at this time. The chant, by the way, is the phrase *Nam M'yoho Renge Kyo*, which Hancock repeats daily for longer periods than it takes to play his LP.] The thought came to me that I had been a musical snob.

For instance I would record any kind of music as long as I was on somebody else's album . . . but when it came to my own album, that had to be unique, special. I was constantly trying to write the great

American masterpiece . . . I didn't know it at the time, but that's where my head was at. I felt the responsibility of the artist is for each guy to try to write the great masterpiece of all time. Well, that's a bit much, and there are very few people capable of doing it. So during the time I was chanting, I started thinking of the great masters I know—Miles Davis, Charlie Parker, John Coltrane, those guys to me, more than anybody else, seem to be the giants of my era—I'm none of those guys, or anywhere near them, so I might as well forget trying to be in that category. Forget trying to be another genius or legend in my own time. Once I got the idea of becoming a genius or legend out of my head, then I felt satisfied in just making some nice music and making people happy. That's what I wanted to do.

I've been trying to get my foot in the door all these years. But I was always trying to do it by disguising. Now the question is: why did I feel it was necessary to disguise these familiar elements? That's what I started asking myself; and that's why I made some changes. I'm beginning to think that what we're doing is, in its own way, as innovative as anything else I've done in the past. I'm finding out that nobody else plays this kind of music this way.

The only three people who've come from the jazz area and got into the funk thing are Donald Byrd, the Crusaders and us. All the other jazz groups that have moved into the popular music areas have gone into either the Latin thing, or rock, or a combination of the two.

Like Chick Corea sounds more rock-Latin . . . and Weather Report is more space music; the popular rhythm element is not funk, r & b . . . it's hard to pin down. Miles definitely is more rock than funk.

L.F.: Now that you've latched on to such a large segment of the American public—the youth public, the rock public, whatever—are there some things you think you can do that you wouldn't have dared do before, in terms of your future plans?

H.H.: Yes, as a matter of fact. I'd like to investigate country music, and see if there's something I can pull out from that and put it in kind of a funk setting that we're working with, with the improvisations on top. Actually, that's what we're trying to do with this current music; we're pulling out elements of funk and r & b. The parts that we feel can fit in the framework of the other music I've been playing, and making what might be essentially a new kind of music. I'm beginning to find out that this is like a new kind of music . . . and it's working. It also might allow other musicians to feel free to work in any area they want to work in. I know how I used to feel, I'd never do this kind of stuff! I've come to find out that there's so much more in the area of rhythm and blues music than I thought before. It's like a completely different language.

L.F.: I think more and more musicians are transcending categories, or combining idioms in such a way that you can't say that this performance is that or the other.

H.H.: Right. I can't call our record jazz; that's misleading. And I can't call it rhythm and blues . . . or rock . . . it doesn't really have a category. When I describe it I have to use my hands to show it's not a clearly defined category. I'm glad that this whole area is being questioned, because it has been used to alienate and segregate types of music, and mislead not only the general public but musicians into falling into that pattern of thinking. I think it's dangerous to think in terms of categories. I really believe that my current success is due in great part to factors beyond the music . . . to all the people at Columbia Records, to my mentor David Rubinson and the Adamsdad Management Company. Columbia thinks I'm going to sell about 600,000 albums, which will mean a gold record. Not even Miles ever got a gold record!

It's funny, Larry Willis of Blood, Sweat & Tears wanted some music, so I sent him a copy of *Chameleon*. David Rubinson said they might record it. I said to David, "Out of sight!" And David said, "Yeah, it's good but of course they don't sell as many records as you do!" That's hard for us to imagine, that I might sell more records than Blood, Sweat & Tears. I'm just stunned by this whole thing."

—MARCH 1974

(*Head Hunters* became a gold record, signifying one million dollars' worth of sales, early in 1975. By late 1975 the album had sold well over 900,000.)

Chick Corea

Somebody out there is listening to Chick Corea. In a recent *Down Beat* readers' poll he was a triple victor: Jazzman of the Year; number one composer (Duke Ellington ran second); number one pianist. His album *Hymn of the Seventh Galaxy* was on the pop charts for months. Much of his success is due to his ability to ally a great talent with a sensitive, recently developed discovery of the art of communication. His quartet, Return to Forever, is by design more accessible than an experimental group called Circle which, about 1971, had the perhaps predictable effect of running around in circles.

"Not enough people could relate to us; we reached a limited audience on a level of intellectualism," said Corea. "They were pleased by the technical brilliance of the performance, though the content and feeling would be a mystery to them. Soon I decided I'd rather create understanding than mystery, so the next move was a return to the roots of music—melody, rhythm and form. It felt right and good and I became aware that this feeling was related to a basic purpose in life that had begun to be rekindled in me, namely the simple desire to reach out and communicate."

The intensity of this ambition is related to Corea's venture into Scientology, beginning with a Communications course in the United States and continuing at the Mother Center outside London, during a long sojourn in England a couple of years ago.

Return to Forever has a standard rock format with an electric rhythm section and aggressive drums. The contemporaneity of its musical language is familiar enough to engage the interest of the typical listener.

"From that point, we have them eased up to the stage where they will listen to anything we care to do. Therefore I have a chance to play acoustic piano solos; Stanley Clarke will switch to his upright bass; we will improvise more, play subtler music."

Corea reached his present goal through circuitous channels. Born in 1941 in Chelsea, Massachusetts, he spent the early 1960s in Latin and Afro-Cuban groups (Mongo Santamaria, Willie Bobo, Herbie Mann) before taking the avant garde-space-rock route and putting in some time with Miles Davis. An articulate, dedicated aesthete, Corea once wrote a series of sensitive essays on the universality of music, and of the degree to which, in his view, masses of listeners look to artists for a lifestyle and a dream of the future.

"There is always a dichotomy between the fine arts and commercialism," he says. "You have creators who function on a very high level, but because of their inability to connect with society, they leave most of the culture ten or twenty years behind. On the other hand, you have a much lower quality of communication, a hyped-up sort of performance which is passed off on people when the motivation is money and record sales. This seems to me to be unnecessary. Too many artists nowadays tend to underestimate their listeners' ability to appreciate finer things.

"Our group has been playing to young rock audiences who are definitely not yet educated in the fine arts, yet their ears and minds are open to quality communication as long as the artists are not aloof. Too often the player has the attitude of 'Well, you don't understand it,' and withdraws into his own universe.

"You have to be really anxious to communicate. If you go to the butcher store and you know Joe the butcher and his ethnic background and what he's into, you won't start off talking to him about nuclear physics. If you really have an affinity for Joe the butcher, regardless of your different cultural origins, it'll be 'Hi Joe, how's the family?', without any feeling of having to butter him up. By the same token, if your motives are pure, you can bring a higher quality art form to people you didn't think you could reach."

Social protest is not part of Corea's scale of values. "I don't feel rebellious at all about being an American. I would just like to contribute, as part of a group called Americans, to the creation of something basic and honest. I am more concerned about using my energies and ability as an artist to improve conditions than to create an art form that would be beautiful in itself without being comprehensive or valuable to a whole society."

With this in mind, Corea and his musicians—the formidable Stanley Clarke on bass, Bill Connors on guitar and Lenny White on drums—find their way to the hearts, souls and feet of listeners.

"If I compare our band with other rock bands, I feel we are quite mature. We smile and have fun, and seeing this, the audience feels good right along with us. We show that no hype is needed, that we don't need to go through all sorts of social machinery in order to get a message across."

It sounds very simple, yet where Corea has succeeded others have failed. The reason could be that the quality of conception and the level of idealism must be at least as high as the manner in which it is communicated.

Extending his horizons along these lines, Corea founded Forever Unlimited Productions in 1973. Its objectives include publishing (a songbook and a series of children's songs), recording (an album under Stanley Clarke's name) and other ventures that will, in his words, "communicate to people of varying cultures and musical ideals."

Perhaps eventually we may even be regaled with a soundtrack album, recorded live at the store in which Corea, after a few months of his clearly infallible softening-up process, engages Joe the butcher in a lively discussion on nuclear physics.   —MARCH 1974

Dave Holland

The overnight stardom phenomenon of show-biz legend seldom happens in jazz. Most leaders and sidemen of any consequence pay months or years of dues before reaching meaningful stature. The case of Dave Holland is a rare exception. Fresh out of Guildhall School of Music, he was fortunate enough to be accompanying a singer one night at Ronnie Scott's Club when Miles Davis, who was vacationing in London, walked in.

Two weeks later the call came from New York. On August 7, 1968 Holland became a member of the most famous and respected of all avant garde jazz combos, the Miles Davis Quintet. Miles was so happy that he couldn't even put on his surly act for me. "How about that Dave?" he said backstage during the group's 1968 concert at UCLA. "Ain't he a bitch?"

"How long did it take you to decide to hire him?" I asked. "Just that one evening?"

"Less than that."

The young man who received this singular honor was born October 1, 1946, in Wolverhampton, England, was raised on a carefully graduated diet: from ukulele (at four) to guitar, and thence to electric bass guitar, which he played in a rock group during his four final school years, before switching to bass fiddle in 1964.

"I always wanted to come to America, but I never dreamed it would happen this way," said Holland, a tall youth with a long, golden beard. "When Miles sent for me, I had only four days to prepare. Luckily I knew most of his music from the records. Right after I got to New York, we opened for ten days at Count Basie's Club in Harlem."

Despite the winds of polarization blowing uptown, Holland says he felt no racial draft: "I guess being with Miles has made me an honorary soul brother. Miles is incredible. I feel such strength flowing from him—he's the kind of man that comes along once in a generation. It's awe-inspiring being around him and these other great players—I feel like I've entered an institution of higher learning. Miles likes to move from one tune to another, without pausing, so we never know what's going to happen next. You've got to be ready to move wherever he goes—usually he'll play an opening phrase that gives just a hint of the next number."

Davis's intuitive ear for talent has not betrayed him. Holland is indeed a phenomenal youngster; his melodic conception is exceptional. If he stays with the group permanently, it is possible that he will emerge as a talent of lasting and influential value to American jazz.

John Lewis's prediction of 1966, that the center of gravity of new jazz talent was moving to Europe, is borne out yet again by the case of Dave Holland. With pianist Joe Zawinul from Vienna contributing so much to Cannonball Adderley's Quintet, guitarist Francois Vaz accompanying Carmen McRae, and youths like violinist Jean-Luc Ponty winning American jazz polls, the evidence mounts: the seeds American jazz planted in Europe soil have produced a flourishing crop.   —OCTOBER 1968

Donald Byrd

The image of the jazz, pop or rock musician as pedant and intellectual has never been readily acceptable to the layman; yet in the past few years many accomplished artists, especially in jazz, have been lured into an academic career.

Donald Byrd is the definitive musician cum laude. Acclaimed in the late 1950s as a young trumpeter on his way to the top, he played with Art Blakey and Max Roach, then led various small combos. During the 1960s, his lifestyle gradually shifted. He became involved in both teaching and studying, ultimately earned an M.A. degree from the Manhattan School of Music, and he immersed himself in Afro-American music, its history and culture. "My fascination with this subject," Byrd said recently, "began with a trip to West Africa, where I saw etchings in caves, showing musicians playing a variety of strange musical instruments. Some of them were estimated to date from 5000 B.C. Recently I recorded a collection of authentic African music, using primitive instruments and the dialects of several tribes."

Byrd is chairman of the Black Music Department at Howard University in Washington, D.C., where most of the students are black. "When I started there in 1968," he said, "I had three classes: musical history, a seminar, and a jazz band. The next semester, I included arranging. I've continued to expand; there are six now, and ultimately I plan to offer as many as eighteen."

Though black Americans are belatedly gaining the opportunity to study their own history, their music is still bought and supported predominately by whites. Ironically, at the first Washington Blues Festival held at Howard, an estimated seventy-five per cent of the crowd in the auditorium consisted of young white hippies.

"Black Music" is of course an omnibus phrase that takes in not only jazz but choral forms (spiritual and gospel); classical works by such Afro-American writers as William Grant Still; pure African music; and the various Caribbean and South American idioms. One of the classes lately added to his curriculum is called "Legal Protection of Literature, Music and Art." His decision to give this course had a remarkable side effect: in 1970, at the age of 37, Byrd enrolled as a student in the law school at Howard. When he wasn't blowing the blues on his horn, or explaining some phrase of music history to the 250 students in his class, he explored the minutiae of torts, contracts, copyrights, federal communications and labor relations. As if this was not enough to take up his time, Byrd accepted concert and lecture engagements around the country, hosted an educational TV series in New York, and continued to record for Blue Note Records. His album, *Electric Byrd,* illustrates how far he could move from African primitivism: it combines all the new textures that modern technology can afford the contemporary musician—feedback, fuzztone, echo, wah-wah, along with a sax section and electric piano.

During his quest for knowledge he was shaken by the discovery that much of the history of Afro-American music has gone unwritten, or is urgently in need of rewriting. The common assumption has been that jazz was baptized in New Orleans around the turn of this century. ''I was talking to a scholar down South, who said he had seen manuscripts by black musicians that go back to the early 1800s, and they were certainly jazz-related. As for the 'Jazz-was-born-in-New Orleans' theory, this is definitely a myth. It's the product of propaganda. Eubie Blake, the ragtime pianist, in his ninth decade, told me about hearing jazz in Baltimore before the 1900s; also I discovered that they had jazz bands in Detroit around the same time. Alain Locke, the philosophy teacher who wrote a book on the Negro contribution to American culture, has talked about the existence in the 19th century of at least six different regions of jazz or black music around the country.'' Byrd found that it was Jelly Roll Morton, the egocentric pianist-composer, whose extravagant claims helped bolster the reputation of New Orleans as a jazz center. ''According to Eubie Blake, if it had been left up to Jelly, the history books would credit him with having written the *Star Spangled Banner.* I enjoy sharing with my students the discovery of all these misapprehensions. There are so many unanswered questions, social as well as musical.

''For example, there was a study around 1910 by H.E. Krehbiel, examining Afro-American folk songs, but it's only recently that the African-derived Gullah language of the Georgia Sea Islands—and that's an historically significant area—has been studied and understood; so what kind of knowledge could this man have possessed? Most of the ethnomusicological data from that era is invalid, and there's much, much more information that has to be dug up.

''It's my dream,'' said Byrd, ''to have the finest ethnomusicology department in the country.'' Given his inquisitive mind and limitless

stamina, his ambition seems very likely to be realized.
—JANUARY 1971

(Because of the unprecedented success of his albums since then, Byrd has given up his post at Howard University in order to resume playing concerts and clubs with his group.)

Supersax

If Charlie Parker had survived the ravages that narcotics, alcohol, racism and other evils imposed on him, he would recently have celebrated (August 29) his 53rd birthday. But the "Bird Lives" phrase has more meaning now than in any year since his death, if only because of the existence of Supersax.

In 1963 Joe Maini, a gifted alto soloist of the Parker school, was working in a Los Angeles band led by a similarly oriented saxophonist, Med Flory. "We had a great reed section," Flory recalls, "and we all dug Bird, so I decided to take the entire improvised solo off his record of *Star Eyes* and harmonize it for a full saxophone section. It took forever to work it out. Then Maini, who had memorized Bird's solo on *Just Friends* note for note, put me to work on writing that one out too. But later, after what happened to Joe, I sort of gave up on the whole idea." What happened to Joe Maini was never pinpointed. He was at a friend's house; there was a revolver around; the official report was accidental shooting, self-inflicted. Like Parker, Maini died at the age of 34.

After an eight-year lapse, a friend named Buddy Clark was at Flory's house and, as Clark remembers it, "I asked Med to bring out that old tape we'd made with Joe. Pretty soon we developed the idea of building a whole library of music out of Charlie Parker solos."

The painstaking job of fanning out Bird's single-note improvised lines into five-way exercises for a reed section was undertaken mainly by Clark, a bassist and arranger from Kenosha, Wisconsin, who had moved to California in the mid 1950s. Flory also wrote some of the arrangements. Next came the even tougher task of finding a group of musicians capable of reading and interpreting the Parker creations faithfully. It took eleven months of rehearsals before a stable personnel was formed, along with enough Bird songs to stretch through an evening at a club.

Supersax made its first public appearance in 1972 at Donte's in North Hollywood. Of the nine members (five saxes, trumpeter Conte Candoli and a rhythm section) only two actually worked with Parker: Jay Migliori, a saxophonist from Boston, and pianist Ronnell Bright. But because the entire band grew up in the bop era, it can tear into a flag-waver like *Ko Ko* or weave through *Parker's Mood, Just Friends* and *Hot House* with total authenticity.

As co-pilot of this enterprise, Med is acting out only one part of the multi-faceted Flory story. Ruggedly handsome, 6 feet 5 inches tall, impressive both in appearance and intelligence, he is a writer of television scripts and has appeared as an actor in more than 150 TV shows, including *Mannix, Ironside, Nichols, Bonanza, Shiloh, The Bold Ones* and the ABC movie of the week, *Home for the Holidays*. He has dozens of motion picture credits, among them *The Nutty Professor* with Jerry Lewis. Industrial films and radio commercials are among his other sources of revenue. He was able recently to effect a two-career parlay when Supersax was hired to do a jingle, with Flory writing the music and speaking the voice-over.

What began as a labor of love (all the members of the band have other jobs, mostly as freelance Hollywood studio musicians) has turned into a surprise hit. Their first LP on Capitol sold close to 30,000 in the first three months, a healthy figure for a pure jazz album rooted in the traditions of the 1940s. An appearance at the Newport Festival/West in Los Angeles broadened their audience, and they were looking forward to a gig at the Monterey Jazz Festival. "That will be our most memorable night," Flory said. "Dizzy Gillespie heard our album, and it seems he really dug the idea and even wanted to play with us. Well, Monterey is having a special evening dedicated to Bird, using music and musicians of his time—the Modern Jazz Quartet, Sonny Stitt, Frank Rosolino, Carmen McRae, Ray Brown, Dizzy's quintet and our band. For a windup we're going to join forces with Diz to play a couple of his best-known compositions, things he and Bird used to play together." Supersax is now so steeped in Parker lore that the infinite subtleties of Bird's phrasing no longer take so long to master. "It's almost like archaeology," Clark said, "putting together the bones of a phrase, figure out what he was trying to say and how he did it. The one that gave me most pleasure to transcribe was *Ko Ko*, because it was my favorite Bird solo when I was seventeen. When we tackle something like that and really get it down, there's a wonderful sense of accomplishment—not just re-creation, but a new form of creation."

Clark had a point. The marvel of Supersax is that it suggests how Charlie Parker might have played if God had given him 10 hands, and the ability to produce four or five-part harmony on the spur of the moment. Ironically, in Bird's day, particularly when he faced a hostile reactionary audience in Los Angeles, his innovations were rejected as radical and unmusical. Today, 18 years after his death, the Parker name is being restored while his compositions and solos are welcomed as part of the mainstream. There is even a Charlie Parker Square in Kansas City ("Bird sure would have dug that," said Flory). As have so many artists through the centuries, Clark, Flory and their colleagues have learned that yesterday's outrage is today's orthodoxy.

The five-way Supersax choruses are an aural analog of the line drawing turned into a statue, or a warped old 78 transformed into glorious quadraphonic sound. In bringing the masterpieces of Charlie Parker to a generation for whom he is at most a dimly remembered name, this ensemble is rendering an invaluable service with loving care.   —SEPTEMBER 1973

OLD MASTERS

Reb Spikes

In a memento-filled apartment on a quiet, grass-sidewalked street in Los angeles there lives a man who could reminisce endlessly and fascinatingly about the music scene in Los Angeles clear back to the early years of this century.

"I've never been on TV," says Benjamin (Reb) Spikes. "Just about everything else in show business, but never television." Reb Spikes is a name you know, if you read your old record labels, as half of the Spikes Brothers. He and his brother John, who died in 1955, shared ASCAP credit for *Someday Sweetheart*, on which the list of recordings (Armstrong, Basie, Bing, Dorsey, Goodman—name anyone) stretches back half a century to the original version by Alberta Hunter, for whom William Grant Still wrote the arrangement.

Spikes carries himself well and speaks proudly of the firsts he achieved, detailing them with a lucidity not common in a man in his eighties. He has been a musician, composer, publisher, agent, store owner, realtor, impresario; you could call him the first major black capitalist ever associated with pop music and jazz. When his family moved to Los Angeles from his native Dallas in 1898, he stood on the street corners selling the *Los Angeles Times*. At thirteen he worked for a tailor shop that pressed *Times* owner General Harrison Gray Otis's clothes every morning.

Though his two brothers and two sisters went to college, Reb's schooling was sporadic. The whole family was musical; one sister became a concert pianist; Reb learned to play sax and clarinet; John took up the trumpet. By 1907 they and a third brother, Richard, who played trombone and guitar, put together a revue, the Spikes Brothers Comedy Show.

"Richard didn't stay with music long. He became a barber by day and an inventor by night. With his inventions—an automobile stick shift, the rear stoplight, all kinds of devices for cars and trains—he made $400,000, but he was always giving his money away or spending it on the next invention, and he died poor. All inventors are kooks, you know.

"John and I had a little circuit and toured Arizona every year, headquartering in Douglas, Ariz. One day in 1910 a carnival stopped over. A young girl who was singing and dancing in the carnival left to join our show. Her name was Hattie McDaniel."

The brothers were running a theater in Muskogee, Oklahoma, when Jelly Roll Morton drifted into town. "Jelly wasn't playing piano then. He was blackening his face for minstrel work, doing comedy. We left town together with McCabe's Troubadors. Pretty soon Jelly, who was always a great braggart, was telling the pianist what to do, and he played so much piano they finally let him do it in the show, along with his minstrel routines." The Morton-Spikes friendship led to several profitable collaborations. Reb and John added lyrics to Jelly's *Wolverine Blues*, a Dixieland standard to this day.

Tiring of the road, the Spikes brothers moved to San Francisco where they led the So Different Band at the So Different Cafe. Reb says, "I was billed as 'The World's Greatest Saxophonist,' and we had the best band in the country; so good that in 1917 when Baron Long, who was running a cabaret in Watts, heard us he canceled the Original Dixieland Jazz Band so he could use us instead." At Baron Long's, where Rudolph Valentino was an obscure exhibition dancer, the headlined entertainer was Harry Richman.

Los Angeles, it seemed, could be a fertile stomping ground for an enterprising black man just after World War I. Settling there permanently in 1919, the brothers opened the Dreamland Cafe and other restaurants and clubs, as well as a music store on Central Avenue. "Our store became a headquarters for Negro musicians. Before long we were supplying bands for the silent movie studios—you know, *Hearts and Flowers* when Cecil B. De Mille wanted a sad scene, things like that. We were paid $2.50 a day. Then the stars began hiring us for parties: Chaplin, Wallace Reid, Fatty Arbuckle. We just somehow grew into a talent agency; we might have seven or eight bands out working for us on the same night."

The growing market for black blues (white stars in chauffeured limousines came by to stock up on "dirty" Race records which the white shops would not sell) convinced Reb and John Spikes that in addition to importing from the East, they ought to try some waxing of their own. "A singer named Nordskog had a recording machine at his home in Santa Monica. Kid Ory, who had moved West from New Orleans, was working in one of our cafes, so we recorded his band."

Released in 1921, *Ory's Creole Trombone* on Sunshine Records had Papa Mutt Carey on cornet; the bass player was Ed "Montudie" Garland, who, in his late seventies, is still playing gigs in Los Angeles. This was the first record by black jazzmen ever released, and probably the first phonograph record of any kind produced in California. Stopping off in Chicago on a promotional tour, Reb caught King Oliver's band. One Oliver sideman, intrigued by the recording project, said "Reb, some day I'm gonna be on records too." This was a classic of understatement, though it would be two years before the first records were released in which Louis Armstrong was heard—as second cornetist in the Oliver band.

"We made several other records," Reb Spikes recalls, "but the wax masters had to be shipped east for processing, and going through the heat of the desert they melted. We had to scrap them." Sunshine Records soon went into a total eclipse, but before long the Spikeses were riding high with "Someday Sweetheart" royalties; a publishing house of their own that put out some blazing blues; and a band called the Majors and Minors, heard for several years at the Follies Theater on Main Street. "Ivie Anderson, who later was with Duke Ellington for ten years, sang and danced with us. We made a little history at the Follies; it was the first time a colored group had been featured in a white show."

In 1924 the brothers wrote the score for *Stepping High*. Reaching into a huge pile of memorabilia, Reb showed me the souvenir program. The title number was billed as "Sung by Mary Richard and Dusky Beauty Chorus." The role of Elder was played by one Eddie Anderson. "Yes," said Reb, "this was Rochester's first appearance in a show." By this time brother John was losing his eyesight. "He couldn't get around much, so he opened a studio and instructed a lot of fine musicians. Then in 1927 Warner Bros. sent for me. With my band and eight or ten acts, we made a forty-five minute sound picture called *Reb Spikes and His Follies Entertainers*. That was in the Vitaphone series, and it came out before *The Jazz Singer*. When it opened, my name was on a big banner across Main Street. Of course, since the sound was recorded separately on disc, it was continually going out of sync. Many years later I tried to get a print of the film, but they told me it had been sold for TV along with 500 others, and today there's no trace of it."

Always alert for new work channels and new talent, Reb Spikes sent to Chicago for a teen-aged drummer recommended to him by Les Hite. "That was Lionel Hampton, and he was already doubling on xylophone. Later Hite had his own band, with Lionel on drums, and that was the group Louis Armstrong fronted at Sebastian's Cotton Club in Culver City."

Everything fell apart for the Spikes Bros. during the Depression years. John's eyes failed completely, though he still wrote music. By 1931, when Reb laid aside his saxophone, the brothers had closed the shop, selling off their record stock at twenty cents a disc. A long siege of illness sidelined Reb for years. The golden Sunshine touch had gone; no longer did he have songs or ideas whose time had come. In 1941 he and Jelly Roll, who had moved to California to regain his fragile health, made plans for a publishing company. "Everything looked good; Jelly was all excited about it. Then just as we were ready to start, a couple of weeks later, doggone, Jelly got sick and died."

An attempt to revive the record company also aborted. Reb became involved in a revue, *Jump, Jive 'n' Jam*. Six months of rehearsal led to a two-week run. In 1950 Reb went into real estate, remaining active until 1962, when, he says, he retired. But the retirement has been far from total. *Someday Sweetheart* and his other copyrights have to be taken care of, as does the property he still owns. Today Reb Spikes, whose heart has belonged to music for eight decades, has a special preoccupation. He has been working for a year on a screenplay, "The Heart and Soul of a Slave," based on the true story of a woman named Biddy Mason (1818-93) who became, as Reb himself became seventy-five years later, a pioneer black capitalist.

"Biddy Mason was brought here from Mississippi by a plantation owner and kept in slavery against the laws of California. There was a trial; she was given her freedom. Working as a nurse, she saved her money and began to buy property; first a lot at 3rd and Spring Streets for $250.—$50. down. Later she bought 1st and Broadway, 1st and Los Angeles, 8th and Hill and many other downtown properties. She eventually arranged for her former slavemaster, who had fallen on hard times, to take a job working for a man who, like Biddy, had once been

his slave. When Biddy died she was a very wealthy woman. It's an in-
spirational story. I wrote ten songs for it, all spirituals. I'm trying to get
a motion picture company interested. It has no nudity, no bed scenes.
Just lots of drama and plenty of wholesome comedy."

I wished the author luck and took my leave, wondering which finally
might turn out to be the more viable screen property: the uplifting saga
of Biddy Mason or the story of Reb Spikes.   —MAY 1972

Barney Bigard

The most irreversible manifestation of obsolescence is one controlled
not by industry, but by fate; human absolescence. The arts develop
their giants, but the noblest expressions of our admiration are usually
reserved for a time when they will be unable to read them. This is a
small attempt to correct that injustice. Barney Bigard is, as they say,
alive, in good health and living in Los Angeles. The keening, swirling
runs of his clarinet, though rarely heard in public now, have lost none
of their limpid beauty. Bigard toured the world with Louis Armstrong
from 1946-55 and again in 1960, but jazz students know him best for
the totally personal sounds he contributed for fourteen years to the
peerless orchestra of Duke Ellington.

The Bigards can trace their lineage back to the mid-18th century.
Some of his ancestors played music for a hobby; many were cabinet-
makers or cigar makers; and if he traded his hawaiian shirt for a business suit, Bigard would look something like one's notion of a Latin-
American brain surgeon. He owes his patrician features to Creole ancestry: French, Spanish and Indian on his mother's side, Negro on his
father's.

Bigard followed the classic pattern of the early jazzmen from New
Orleans to Chicago ("King Oliver sent for me in 1925") to New York,
where he played with Oliver and Luis Russell before joining Duke in
January, 1928.

Moving west in 1942, he spent two years with Freddie Slack ("The greatest boogiewoogie pianist of them all!''), had his own group and worked for the trombonist Kid Ory, who in his eighties now lives in comfortable retirement in Honolulu collecting royalties from *Muskrat Ramble*. Bigard's situation is similar to Ory's. As co-composer of *Mood Indigo* (the second melody is his, following a main theme written by Ellington) he has a good income from ASCAP, which could have been far greater but, because musicians for many years remained largely uninformed about their rights, he did not become a member until 1956—26 years after *Mood Indigo* was written. ''Jazzmen were young and foolish and didn't know the business end of music,'' he said without rancor. ''Nobody knew anything about copyrighting songs. Publishers and bandleaders would buy outright, for $25, tunes that later earned tens of thousands.''

Another tune that grew out if the Ellington band was *Rockin' In Rhythm*. Bigard recalled: ''We were working at a theater, backing up Pigmeat Markham in a comedy routine. I said to Johnny Hodges, 'Why don't we figure out something to play behind him?' That's how the *Rockin' In Rhythm* melody began.'' The ASCAP Biographical Dictionary lists *Rockin' In Rhythm* and *C Jam Blues* as Bigard's compositions though he says neither label credit nor income ever accrued to him. (The book credits Ellington, too, with both tunes; Duke also orchestrated them for the band.)

He remembers the Ellington years as a period of constant stimulus and creativity. Its personnel was composed of a now vanishing breed of individualists. ''In the early years the morale in the band was high; people commented about how wonderful the guys dressed, and we all showed up on time. The entire orchestra was made up of great soloists. Duke was very smart. If he wrote a number for me, he'd study me; he knew my style and capacity, knew exactly what I could do, and he'd tailor the tune to fit me like a glove.'' In 1936 Bigard was the subject of the first jazz composition every built around a single soloist. Composed by Ellington and Bigard, it was known as *Clarinet Lament* or *Barney's Concerto*. With it, Ellington set a pattern imitated by jazz composers for the past 32 years.

That jazz reached such creative peaks during the 1930s was the more remarkable when one considers the conditions under which its geniuses worked and traveled. So many hotels were off limits to Negroes that the band had its own Pullman car and literally had to live on the train. Restaurants being equally inaccessible, the band valet was sent out for whatever scrubby sandwiches he could find. ''For days on end, we'd stop at the railroad yards where everybody would spray water on one another and we'd soap ourselves down and take a bath.'' One night, at an all-white date in Birmingham, Alabama, the band was segregated from the audience by a line of policemen. When a scuffle developed in the hall, the cops had to leave the bandstand temporarily unguarded, whereupon a white youth sprang up and addressed himself to Bigard and to Juan Tizol, the pale-skinned Puerto Rican trombonist. ''What are you two white guys doing, playing in this nigger band?'' he demanded. ''We told him we were just in it for the money,'' says Bigard, ''and that seemed to satisfy him.''

Jim Crow aside, Bigard worked under two other shadows: that of the mob and in later years the imminence of World War II. ''Ellington was at the Cotton Club in Harlem for all those years, but the crime syndicate in charge wanted Negroes there strictly as entertainers, not as customers. They made a few exceptions like 'Bojangles' Robinson, who had a lot of power and carried his own gun. Some of the small-time hoodlums were resentful of a man like Duke having all that money. When the band doubled between the Cotton Club and a theater, a gangster bodyguard with a machine gun between his legs accompanied Duke while he commuted in a limousine. In Chicago, Duke was again threatened with extortion. Some of the big boys called Owney Madden for him and Madden contacted Al Capone. Capone sent out two guys who hid behind posts in the lobby at Duke's hotel and stopped the hoods from going upstairs and taking his loot.''

During the band's European tour in the spring of 1939, the late Rex Stewart, Duke's cornetist, headed up a record date in Paris. ''We wanted Django Reinhardt and a French drummer, but neither of them showed up. They finally found Django, but he had lost his guitar. Somebody picked another one up for him, and it was all unglued in back, but somehow he got it together, tuned it and played like mad. I had to double on drums for that date.'' (The session became an often-reissued classic.) ''A few days later, the band was crossing from Holland into Germany, and an Englishman said to us: 'You see those haystacks in the fields? Behind all of them there's machine gunners.' We were crossing a bridge and hoping it wouldn't be dynamited. Luckily we got out of Germany fast, canceled plans to return to Paris and hurried home.''

Bigard's departure from the band in 1942 left a gap that was never filled. Jimmy Hamilton, who held the clarinet chair for twenty-six years before quitting, is an academic musician in the Goodman tradition—"a fine musician, but not a jazzman," says Bigard. The deep, rich warmth of Barney's lower register, the soaring flights of his high notes, the unique capacity for bending a tone so slowly that you could spin a dime on it, these were qualities that others envied but none could accurately duplicate. Barney recalls the Armstrong period as one of musical freedom. "Because it was a small group, I got to play more. It was quite a contrast from all those soloists I shared time with in the Ellington band. The African tour in 1960 was a trip to remember. We knew there were primitive areas in the bush country, but we found the cities pretty much like our own. The music had changed, too—they even had Dixieland bands in nightclubs, and got us to sit in with them. Just one night, near Accra, Ghana, they put on a special show of native music for us. It was all percussion, no melody instruments, and you could hear the relationship to jazz. They have good rhythm," said Creole Barney Bigard, without tongue in cheek, of his African cousins.

Since quitting the road in 1961, he has found little to stimulate him on the musical scene. He keeps in only partial contact with new developments and was intrigued when I played him a record of an amplified saxophone. He has witnessed the decline of jazz clarinet, which he attributes to the technical challenge of the instrument. His respect is reserved for a few of the pioneers. "To me, the greatest player that ever lived was Artie Shaw. He created tunes of his own. Benny Goodman played pop songs; he didn't produce new things like Shaw did." Of his fellow New Orleanians, he observes: "Johnny Dodds was a limited musician. Jimmie Noone was much more polished. Today, there's Pete Fountain—he has a style, but you still hear that Goodman concept behind it, and he can't improve on Goodman. I always tell the youngsters, don't copy anybody. Learn from them, then improve and become yourself."

For several years Bigard has worked only occasionally—when the money was right, the company good, and, if driving was involved, the location close. ("I just refuse to ride those freeways.") He played the Monterey Dixieland Festival and a recent educational TV show in Chicago. He may work again tomorrow or not for a year. Living quietly with his second wife, Dorothe (they were married just after he left Ellington). Bigard putters around the apartment, watches the ball games and visits with his children, all four of whom live in California. He is loved and has a good life; if there are a few regrets, he feels that bitterness and remorse are counter productive.

Born in 1906, first married at seventeen, Albany Leon Bigard is twelve times a grandfather and talks proudly of his baby great-grand-daughter. None of his descendants is in music, which suits him fine. He has seen too much of the rigors in the life of a peripatetic jazzman. "I often asked Louis Armstrong, 'Pops, why don't you ever get off the road and take a vacation? You can afford it.' But he's always worried that his chops will soften up." Barney Bigard sipped his gin on the rocks, leafed through a music magazine and smiled reflectively. "It's a funny thing. The other night I had a dream. I was on this train and I was cooking for Duke. Cooking like we used to, on a camp stove in the baggage car. He got real mad at me. he said, 'You're putting too much seasoning in it. You're fired.' I wonder what that meant?

"Anyhow, today, if a job comes along, I thank God I'm in a position where I don't have to worry about who hires or fires me. I think I've earned the right to say no."   —JULY 1968

Joe Venuti

"Hey, Joe, tell us about the time that sax player's foot-tapping bugged you and you nailed his shoe to the bandstand."

"Joe, where was it that you heaved the piano out of the hotel window and made book on what note it would hit?"

The scene is the musicians' waiting room at the Broadmoor Hotel in Colorado Springs. A half dozen younger jazzmen sit around fascinated as Joe Venuti weaves his tales (who knows where fact ends and embellishment begins?) of his life as a practical joker.

The man and the musician are totally at odds with one another. Listening to his rasping, godfather voice, watching his waddling walk and potbellied figure, you would never guess that this man is one of the few certified geniuses of jazz, along with a handful of others like Armstrong, Tatum and Bix; or that he had just earned the greatest standing ovation at Dick Gibson's jazz party at the Broadmoor, outpacing men half his age, displaying superb craftsmanship in the ballads, swinging ferociously on the up tempos, now and then wrapping the threads of the bow around his violin in a technique that enables him to play an entire solo in four-note chords.

He has been doing this since the days with Paul Whiteman, Red Nichols, the Dorsey Brothers and a famous recording group called Joe Venuti's Blue Four, whose records were so far ahead of their day that they sound undated almost a half century later.

How does he keep in shape after all these years? Joe, a formally trained musician and expert technician, replies: "I practice two hours a day. Classical music, exercises. And I play golf."

How is his golf game? "I shoot my age." Not bad, when you consider that his age is 79, going on 80. Of course, even this datum is in dispute, since Venuti likes nothing better than to put on men who interview him. For decades he maintained that he was born aboard a ship that was bringing his parents from Italy to the United States on September 1, 1904. Vital statistics were later dug up in the town of Lecco, Italy, where Joe sometimes allows he was born on December 3, 1894. Born into a family of sculptors, he was brought to the United States around 1905, raised in Philadelphia, where he became a school colleague of Eddie Lang, the guitarist who was his partner on a hundred superb records, and a close friend until Lang died in 1933.

Joe's life in music has had five main phases. As the first acknowledged genius of jazz violin, he enjoyed world renown among collectors, recording most often with small chamber groups, and paying a triumphant visit to England in 1934. Throughout much of the swing era he led a less than preeminent big band. He spent a decade working mainly as a studio musician in Hollywood and once had a regular stint on KNXT radio. Then came a fallow period when, except for work in Las Vegas and Seattle, he rarely emerged and was all but forgotten by the jazz community. The fifth stage began in 1961, when he took his last drink. "My stupidity cost me one happy marriage. After I quit the booze, it took me a year to get to understand people. Now I enjoy life a thousand times more."

During the years of oblivion, he drank and gambled his way through three years in Las Vegas. "They kept raising my salary but I could never catch up—I was always in hock to the casino. Finally Bing Crosby bailed me out. Bing has been a great friend; he's a marvelous man, a real humanitarian. I went to Paris with him; I did all those shows for Chesterfield with him; and of course I've known him since we were both with Whiteman in 1929."

Venuti made the transition from classical music to jazz very early. He was aware of the existence of a new, syncopated idiom even before the word jazz was applied to it. "We just called it music with a beat; the word jazz was taboo."

His career as a recording jazz musician began in 1926, when he waxed two duets with Eddie Lang, *Stringing the Blues* and *Black and Blue Bottom*. There followed a series of masterworks most of which grew out of the need to escape from the confines of such big bands as those of Whiteman, Jean Goldkette and Roger Wolfe Kahn. (During their summer hiatus Venuti and Lang would often put a band of their own together to play in Atlantic City.)

His associates during his years as an emerging jazzman were the elite of the white jazz world at the time when segregation was all but total: the Dorseys, Beiderbecke, Hoagy Carmichael, Lennie Hayton, Jack and Charlie Teagarden, Benny Goodman, Bud Freeman. The vocalist on several songs recorded by Venuti's Rhythm Boys was Harold Arlen.

As Venuti, affected by the stress on swing music, became one of a score of second-grade maestros playing one-night stands, his career as a jazz recording artist came to a halt; and the legend of Venuti the incurable prankster outshadowed the reputation of the master musician.

There was a time when he was on an early TV show sponsored by a hair cream. In the middle of a live commercial he bent over, showed his big bald spot to the camera, and said: "This is what that cream oil did for me." The sponsor dropped the show.

And there was the night when, just for the hell of it, he called up thirty-seven bass fiddle players, told each of them to meet him at 7 p.m. at 52nd and Broadway, and then drove around the block enjoying the sight of the sidewalk cluttered with bemused bassists. (At a recent retelling, it was forty-seven tuba players, and the meeting place was Hollywood and Vine. Whatever the details, Joe says: "It got me in trouble with the union. I had to pay each of those guys $18.")

In 1936, Joe's band played the Texas centennial in Dallas opposite Paul Whiteman, who started the show with the stadium in darkness, except for a small spotlight on him while he conducted *The Star Spangled Banner* with a lighted baton. Venuti bribed the electrician to throw a spot on him instead. What the audience saw that night was Joe, dressed only in long underwear, conducting his band with a fishing pole with an electric light bulb on its end.

One night an alto sax player tried out for Venuti's band. Joe kept him waiting around most of the evening, then finally said, "Okay, kid, take a chorus." The saxophonist stood up and played one chorus, then another, and another. Venuti kept him playing for twenty minutes until his eyes were almost popping out of his head, and he found himself repeating the same licks endlessly. Finally Venuti said, "All right, kid, now go out and change my tire."

A typical example of Joe's easily strained patience was the incident at the Lakeside Golf Club in Hollywood when, after hitting a ball into the water several times, he threw the club into the lake, hurled the rest of the bag after it, picked up the caddie and threw him in, and then jumped in himself.

And there is the celebrated story about Wingy Manone, the one-armed trumpeter, to whom Venuti sent a Christmas present—one cuff link.

One hopes that such anecdotes will now recede as the legend of Venuti as musician returns to center stage. His comeback, hindered by a lack of confidence, began slowly. In 1963 he was to record an album for Columbia, his first in many years, but backed out at the last minute; and his place was taken by the late Stuff Smith. But within a few years George Wein, noting his undiminished talent and availability, used him at Newport and on a world tour.

Though his home is in Seattle, where his second wife has worked for Boeing for some twenty-seven years, Venuti during the 1970s has spent most of his time abroad. He has relatives from New Orleans to Boston to Italy. "While I was married to Sally, we had four children and adopted two more. I have twenty-three grandchildren and a great-grandchild on the way. I have a cousin in Lecco, my home town. I was back there again not long ago, and as usual I had to give $50 apiece to relatives and old friends—people who say they knew my father and grandfather—and play free concerts for them.

"I can do things in Europe that I can't accomplish here. I wrote a violin concerto that included some of my early jazz compositions, but couldn't get any American record company interested. I went to Rome, told an executive about it, and he said: 'When do you want to start rehearsing?' Presto! I had 106 men. Of course, I had to take care to show them how to phrase the 'music. Classical violinists don't realize that people like me have something they don't have: the ability to improvise. All they can do is sit there and read the music.''

Venuti has changed little with the years, except that he now plays an amplified instrument. ''A couple of months ago my violin was stolen—a 1697 Seraphin. I miss it; but of course nowadays with an amplifier you can play on a cigar box and it won't sound any different.''

Of his fellow jazz violinists, still few in number, he says: ''I like Stephane Grappelli. That young fellow Jean-Luc Ponty [the avant garde violinist with Mahavishnu John McLaughlin], he's a good musician but I don't understand what he's trying to do.''

After nine months' absence, Joe went back home to Seattle, but had made plans to embark on a tour of Germany with the Dutch Swing College Band. Asked whether he would be home in time to celebrate his 80th birthday, he said: ''No, that's the day after the tour ends. I'll be in Milan. Thank God my wife understands me; she knows I can't sit still. Music even helps to cure my ulcers. Just pick up the violin and the pain goes away.''

Venuti growled a few goodbyes as he made his way back to the Broadmoor bandstand. Within minutes, accompanied by an all-star sextet, he was bringing another crowd to its feet—another triumph in a lifetime dedicated to musicianship of the highest order.

—OCTOBER 1974

Eubie Blake

''People say I'm drunk all the time,'' said Jamie Hubert (Eubie) Blake, ''because I stagger. People are quick to say musicians are drunkards. You'd better tell them—I don't drink anything. It's my arthritis.'' Eubie Blake's arthritis is a minor handicap. At a party held recently in his honor, he had a southpaw handshake for everyone, but the right hand came miraculously to life when, later in the afternoon, he was persuaded to sit at the piano and play a few of his own compositions.

He didn't get around to *Charleston Rag*, which he wrote in 1899. Nobody can be expected to have total recall.

Eubie can safely claim to be the senior ragtime pianist among that dwindling breed. He was born February 7, 1883, in Baltimore. His mother disapproved of all secular music, but around the turn of the century "little Hubie" was skipping out, putting on long pants, jumping over the back fence and playing far into the night at Aggie Shelton's house-of-considerable-repute in the Tenderloin. He outlived those salad days to become a respected vaudevillian, teamed with Noble Sissle, who was his songwriting partner in *I'm Just Wild About Harry*, *Love Will Find A Way* and the other hits that kept the all-black revue *Shuffle Along* on Broadway for eighteen months in 1921-22.

Trim, alert and delightfully garrulous, Eubie Blake is an unquenchable fountain of memories. Ask him about some long-forgotten musician or song, and he will find a link that binds him to each period of the past: "Sure I can remember writing *Poor Jimmy Green*—that was the week after Battling Nelson took the lightweight championship from Joe Gans in 1908."

Who was the kingpin of them all? "Well Art Tatum was out there by himself, of course, but the greatest I ever heard was One Leg Willie. Willie's mother worked for some very rich white people, so they sent him to Boston Conservatory; he was a concert pianist and the only Negro to graduate from his class. His name was Willie Joseph; he was an expert skater and he fell and had to have his leg amputated. One Leg Willie and me, we'd go to somebody's house to play, and he'd start something classical and they'd say. 'Come on man, play something boogie.' He got disgusted and changed from classics to ragtime. In those days Negro musicians weren't even supposed to read music. We had to pretend we couldn't read; then they'd marvel at the way we could play shows, thinking we'd learned the parts by ear. The only arrangement I ever copied from anybody was One Leg Willie's *Stars and Stripes Forever*. He did it in march time, ragtime and '16,' which was later known as boogie-woogie. He played it at contests in Tammany Hall and the old Madison Square Garden, then brought down the house with it at a huge competition organized by the *Police Gazette*."

Having outlived the ragtime craze, which began to fade a half-century ago, Eubie Blake has survived all but a couple of his contemporaries. His income from ASCAP keeps him going, along with an undimmed interest in the spinning-wheel music world around him. Recently John Hammond, Columbia Records' pioneer talent scout brought him into the studio to record a double LP album, his first in years. Noble Sissle rejoined him for some of the vocal numbers; the rags are played solo.

Eubie, who recently took the train back to New York after visiting old friends in Los Angeles, will be wheeling his way back west in December. "Stanley Adams, the president of ASCAP, has invited me to be the guest of honor at a banquet. I'm the second oldest member of ASCAP. The oldest is Rudolf Friml, and the party will be for his 90th birthday. Now, before I forget it again, let me play that *Baltimore Toodle-O* for you."

He sat at the upright piano, and suddenly the California sunshine vanished. It was dark, the light turned red, and Eubie, a small boy in borrowed long pants, was back at Aggie Shelton's moonlighting from high school. I blinked, and there was the old man, his arthritic hands skating over the keys like One Leg Willie over the ice. He finished the number, turned to the small circle of friends and smiled. "Now," he said, "let me tell you about this fellow Jimmy Green, the syncopating march king. When I was in Baltimore in 1896—no, wait a minute, that was 1895 . . ."   —AUGUST 1969

(Blake has since succeeded the late Rudolf Friml as ASCAP's oldest member. In 1973, at the age of 90, he took his first plane trip. During the next three years he made several visits, by air, to California and Europe for television shows and jazz festivals.)

Earl "Fatha" Hines

The manner in which the public deals with its most gifted artists is, to understate it, erratic. Many have gone through the famous-forgotten-famous cycle, but few have achieved a comeback as triumphant and long-lasting as that of the master Earl "Fatha" Hines. One of the fistful of history's great jazz pianists, Hines lapsed into relative obscurity in the early 1960s in San Francisco until, as a result of a couple of concerts in New York, he was "rediscovered" by critics who should never have forgotten him. Since then he has been on a round of festivals, clubs, record dates and concert recitals all over the world.

"People wonder why I use a saxophonist, a singer and a combo instead of working alone," he remarked during a recent visit to Los Angeles' Playboy Club. "Well, I carry these people because it takes some of the weight off me. The way conditions are in night clubs, it puts too much of a strain on you to work a whole show on your own. I'm tired of having to insult people, having to say 'Quiet! Quiet!' I'm tired of people starting up conversations, shouting and laughing while I'm trying to play. What do they come to the club for anyway? That's why I'm glad when I'm finished with my part of the show and the rest of my group comes on. Of course, in Europe it's different. People there pay a lot of attention, which naturally inspires me, whereas on jobs like this I just become bored."

By the end of 1974 Hines, whose glistening, incisively rhythmic keyboard statements came to global attention in a series of records with Louis Armstrong's original Hot Five, had spent eight of the twelve months out of the country, and less than two of the remaining four at his home in Oakland, California. "I was jumping around Europe all summer. When I got back, I was off again to South America, in a piano package show with Marian McPartland, Teddy Wilson and Ellis Larkins. Next week I'm leaving for Europe again to tour for George Wein. He insisted on putting me with a big band, so that's the way it'll be set up; and we'll have Dizzy, Sarah and Billy Eckstine on the same bill."

Wein's thinking is logical. For twenty years Hines led an orchestra, whose members at one point, in 1943, included Charlie Parker and Gillespie, with Sarah Vaughan and Eckstine as vocalists. The European bookings were fashioned to evoke what have come to be known as "the Parker years," with Sonny Stitt recreating the role of Bird. This reunion with some of "Fatha's" children made good musical sense aside from the nostalgia value.

"After that tour," Hines said, "I go to Italy by myself for some solo work; then come back, pick up my combo and go to Japan. Come to think of it, I'm not just tired of night clubs. I'm just plain tired. I need to go some place for about two months and never look at a piano. All this running back and forth across time zones, eating strange food—

there's only so much you can take. The audiences are beautiful, we stay in the best hotels and travel first class, but still there comes a time when you realize that you have everything except what you need most—a chance to relax.''

This typical success syndrome has dogged him for several years. He is in continual demand for record sessions. He could tour fifty-two weeks a year playing concerts only or devote the entire year to playing clubs. Asked whether he welcomed the prospect of touring with an orchestra again, for the first time since he broke up his band in 1947, Earl said: ''For this one short tour I don't mind; but in general it's impractical nowadays. I love the big band sound, but there's no housing for it any more. You can't spend two weeks at a theatre in St. Louis, then a couple of weeks in Miami, the way it used to be. In those days you could hang up your clothes and get some laundry done. Today, the way those one nighters are booked in order to keep a band organized, my gracious, how can someone like Count Basie stand it? It's tough enough for me, when I only have a small group to worry about.''

Trim as an athlete, the picture of health. Hines at 68 looks twenty years younger. He explains: ''Years ago, when I was an amateur boxer, Joe Louis and I were close friends. I'd go with him to Pompton Lakes where he was in training, and watch him do his calisthenics. I've continued to exercise ever since.'' How about practicing? ''I carry my music with me, and once in a while I'll pick out a few things and maybe run down to a piano in the afternoon, but usually I'm lucky to find a bed, let alone a piano.''

As an aftermath to this interview, Hines took his own advice. He called up his agent and asked him to make no commitments for the next couple of months. It is fortunate that he made the decision freely. Back around 1967 Louis Armstrong spoke to me along identical lines (in fact, he talked seriously of taking a six-month sabbatical); but when he finally got off the road it was not a matter of choice; Satchmo was rushed to a hospital.

At this point in his life no audience—in Barcelona, Istanbul or Tokyo, in Zagreb or Zurich—could forget Hines if he stays away for a while. This most respected of pianists has certainly earned time off from an eventful career whose greatness has not only given joy to thousands but inspired the young Stan Kenton, the teen-aged Nat King Cole and other pianists by the thousands with the renowned innovations that established him as the first worldwide influence in his field.

—DECEMBER 1974

Hoagy Carmichael

"If I were unknown," said Hoagy Carmichael, "and if I brought *Stardust* or *Lazy River* or *Rockin' Chair* to a record company today, as unfamiliar material, I wouldn't get past the front door."

Artistic disenchantment aside, Hoagland Howard Carmichael is suffering no discernible malaise. When not relaxing at the Thunderbird Country Club in Palm Springs, he can be found in a compact townhouse near Beverly Hills on the Sunset Strip that serves as a combination office and storehouse of memorabilia.

Composed and suave in white-on-white tie and shirt, he defies you to believe that it is three quarters of a century since his birth in Bloomington, Indiana. About forty-seven years ago a disoriented Carmichael was soaking up bootleg liquor during a Bix Beiderbecke record session. "Where are you going, Hoagland?" he recalls asking himself. "Hot jazz, hot trumpet, music, blues, stomps aren't for you as a career. The law is noble . . . a lawyer finds security and position. That's how a fat cat gets into the exclusive country club and plays golf in the afternoon." In those words, Hoagy reconstructed the dilemma in his autobiography, *Sometimes I Wonder*. Ironically, he now lives precisely in the style to which he once believed the law would gain him access. For a while he was indeed a lawyer, but that career was brief; his place on the periphery of hot jazz became too frustrating.

Though never a world-beater as pianist, cornetist or singer, he had an uncanny gift for putting a melody together. The respect he earned among his hornblowing contemporaries meant more to him than anything else. For a while, outside a basement apartment in West Palm Beach, Florida, his plaque could be seen: "Hoagland Carmichael, Esq., Attorney at Law." He had left his *Washboard Blues* with publisher Irving Mills in New York, but was resigned to a life for which he had no heart.

"Music hardly entered my head for a while until two members of the Wolverines came through town and asked me to join them on drums for a ten-day cruise to Havana. I'd never played drums in my life, but I took the job. After that trip I wrote a crazy thing called *One Night in Havana*, the first North American rhumba. Then one day, early in 1927 in a record shop near my law office, I heard the sound of *Washboard Blues* played by Red Nichols and his Five Pennies. I had no idea they'd recorded it. That did the trick. I'd been making $50 a month as a law clerk, plus whatever business I could pick up on my own. Red's record was all the incentive I needed to go north again.''

Soon he was back among the young Turks with whom he empathised—Bix and Frank Trumbauer, Joe Venuti and Eddie Lang, Don Redman and Louis Armstrong. Over dinner at Redman's house in Detroit he responded to an inquiry about his activities by pulling out the manuscript of a new instrumental work with no words except the title, *Stardust*. ''I wasn't sure what it meant, but it just seemed like a nice title.'' Redman recorded it in October of 1928, at a fairly busy tempo, in a far from sentimental mood. The tune passed next to Jean Goldkette's Detroit band, thence to Victor Young, a violinist with Isham Jones's popular New York dance orchestra. ''Jones wanted to make a record of *Trees* and he decided to put 'Stardust' on the other side. By doing it as a slow melodic tune, featuring Young's violin, he turned it into a hit. Then Mitchell Parish was called in to add lyrics. Louis Armstrong recorded the vocal version in 1931. Bing Crosby picked it up when he was at CBS, and we were on our way.''

Carmichael's association with Armstrong benefited both men. Hoagy had been an acolyte on the early black jazz scene ever since Satchmo came to Chicago to play in King Oliver's band. A recording manager at Okeh suggested that Louis and Hoagy team up for a duet vocal on *Rockin' Chair*, with Hoagy singing the father role and Satch the son. Interracial vocal teams were unheard of in 1929, but the record sold both to blacks and to the white Armstrong fans who were beginning to proliferate. ''The following year,'' says Hoagy, ''I realized a fantastic ambition, recording *Rockin' Chair*, *Georgia* and a couple of others with an all-star band I put together. Bubber Miley and Bix on horns, Tommy Dorsey, Benny Goodman, Bud Freeman, Joe Venuti, Eddie Lang, Gene Krupa—just about everyone I could dream of.'' But it was still a little while before he could find enough security in music to become its officially adopted child. Early in 1931 he and Bix commiserated with each other; Hoagy was working for an investment banking house while Bix, who would die a few months later at twenty-eight, was between gigs.

One night a friend took Carmichael to hear Sidney Arodin, a young New Orleans clarinetist. Arodin had written a melody that enchanted Hoagy, who soon added a verse, fitted it up with a lyric, and titled it ''Lazy River.'' Louis Armstrong recorded it in November of 1931. It has been carrying the Mills Brothers, and vice versa, for better than forty years, and was sung by Hoagy in 1946, in the film, *The Best Years of Our Lives.*

With four Class A hits to his credit, Hoagy revelled not only in financial security, but in the belated realization that he had leaped from obscurity to Broadway celebrity within a three-year span. Given the pace of communications in pre-Repeal years, this was comparable to the thunderbolt success in the 1960s of Lennon-McCartney and Jim Webb.

After *Stardust* had hit a 100,000 copy sale, its composer was offered a $25. weekly drawing account against royalties. Sensing that this was not the best of all possible deals, he checked with another Tin Pan Alley denizen, the publisher of *Rockin' Chair.* In return for a magnificent guarantee of $135. a week, Hoagy willingly tossed *Georgia* into the kitty.

During the more than four decades since the ascent to standard status of his original blockbusters, all four have held up, often reinforced by unexpected new hit versions. In 1960-61 the Si Zentner *Lazy River* and Ray Charles's *Georgia,* neither of which the composer or publisher knew about until they had been recorded, gave both songs a 99-year lease on life. "Young people all over the world have suddenly discovered *Georgia,*" Carmichael says.

In 1951 he finally landed an Academy Award. The film was *Here Comes The Groom,* the performers were Bing Crosby and Jane Wyman, introducing the prize-winning *In the Cool, Cool, Cool of the Evening* (lyrics by Johnny Mercer), certainly not the song by which Carmichael's name will be transmitted to posterity.

"In the late 1950s." he says, "I began to get quite discouraged. Until that time I could go most any place and say, 'listen to this new thing of mine' and they'd listen. But after rock 'n' roll started, I never even got a phone call from an A & R man about anything. Sonny Burke, the record producer, once told me, 'What they write and sing may sound to you like simple stuff, and junky, but I don't think you could write it. It wouldn't sound right, coming from you.' Nevertheless I still write as well as I ever did." The words were spoken neither bitterly nor in defiance of a changing world but as a demonstrable statement of fact.

There have been other disappointments. In 1968 Carmichael taped a one-hour TV special in Sweden with a brilliant cast headed by Svend

Asmussen, the Danish jazz violinist and vaudevillian. "It's a great show, but they can't sell it in this country, because it's in black and white, and everybody's buying only color shows." However, at the end of 1971, he appeared on the premiere TV show of Henry Mancini's series with Bing Crosby, than undertook a straight acting role in the television drama, *Owen Marshall,* opposite Peggy Lee.

Divorced since 1955, Carmichael lives alone. Hoagy Junior, in his thirties, formerly a broker, is a producer for educational television. Randy, two years his junior, plays the piano and sings at a hotel just outside of Chicago. His father collaborated with him in a couple of songs, but, says Hoagy Senior, "he got discouraged; he just couldn't get them recorded. Randy's in the same position as I." ASCAP's King Carmichael still writes songs, demand or no demand. He just completed one with Johnny Mercer, *Fleur-de-Lis,* to be recorded by Tony Bennett.

"Many years ago," Hoagy said, "I played tennis with George Gershwin, and after the game we got to talking about songs. We shook hands and solemnly agreed we'd never write a Hawaiian song. Well, two of my recent tunes are *Hawaii, Pearl of the Sea,* recorded by Roger Williams, and *Hawaiian Evening Song,* which I hope maybe Don Ho will sing."

He turned to the phonograph, flipped on a 78, and the low-roofed sunlit room was filled with the crystal pure cornet of Bix playing some forgotten tune Hoagy wrote for him. "Listen to the beauty of that," cried Hoagy. "Was there ever anyone else like Bix?"

The thought crossed my mind that Hoagy himself, as much as the rarest Bix record, is a collector's item, one of a kind—a still-involved, lively monument to an era no period TV musical can ever reconstruct.

—APRIL 1973

Red Norvo

For the performing musician, there is only one nightmare more horrendous to comtemplate than paralysis of the hands, and that is deafness.

Red Norvo, an inspiration to xylophone and vibes players since he introduced the mallet family to jazz about four decades ago, had to face the specter earlier this year. Nearing the end of a European concert tour for Pan American Airways and the U.S. Travel Service, Norvo revealed the extent of his ordeal, which had still not leaped the final hurdle.

"You know I always had some slight trouble with my ears," he said, "as a result of a mastoid infection when I was a child. Well, it never bothered me seriously and I didn't know that there were lesions, which grew worse through the years. One evening I was working in Palm Springs when the group was playing *I Concentrate on You*. It was in the key of E Flat, but suddenly I noticed to my horror that I had somehow wandered into the key of D. I was hearing everything a half tone flat: the vibrations coming through to me were unable to push the tone up to where it belonged. I realized I actually couldn't hear what the band was playing. I got off the bandstand and went home to Santa Monica. It was frightening. I didn't play another note for months."

After lying low at home with his wife (sister of composer Shorty Rogers), Norvo underwent an operation on his left ear which, he says, "the doctor just about rebuilt for me." The ear soon began to vibrate again, though undependably. "I have good days and bad days. Some people's voices are much easier to understand than others. There are days when I hear pretty well and others, especially if I catch a cold, when it's real rough. Through all the trouble I got some wonderful moral support from Nanette Fabray. She told me, 'I had three operations. Don't give up—be patient!' I have about sixty percent hearing in each ear now. I'm supposed to have another operation on the right ear and possibly the left, too. But I may wait awhile."

During his four weeks in Europe, Norvo played first in England with a mainstream group, the Newport All Stars, with George Wein at the piano, Ruby Braff on trumpet, Barney Kessel on guitar and Benny Carter on alto saxophone. During the rest of the tour he was accompanied by two young modern musicians, guitarist Jerry Hahn and bassist Steve Swallow, borrowed from the Gary Burton Quartet. On some concerts he played vibes duets with Burton to mutually stimulating effect. Norvo's unfailing good taste and ability to work with representatives of every school of jazz served him well again. At most of his appearances he received the biggest hand of the evening.

Even sixty-percent of those ovations, penetrating the damaged ears, must have been enough to offer the encouragement he needed. Norvo is a true giant of jazz, beloved by his peers, respected by his juniors.

Now that the restoration of his hearing is virtually assured, we look forward to sharing in his good fortune. It can only be hoped that the area of his activities, confined for too many years to the Nevada lounges, will be expanded to include many of this country's surviving jazz rooms.

It's about time, too, that some musically sensitive A & R man put him back on records after all these years. The record companies, it would seem, suffer from a worse hearing problem than Norvo ever faced: they have cash registers for eardrums.   —NOVEMBER 1968

(After the death of his wife in July 1972, Red Norvo went into complete retirement for a year. Since 1973 he has been active, playing concerts and festivals in the States and abroad, his hearing sufficiently restored to enable him to function normally.)

Jess Stacy

Retirement is not a word you associate with jazz musicians. Louis Armstrong was aching to get back on the stand until the final day of his illness. Lil Armstrong died at the keyboard playing a memorial for Satch a few weeks later. Duke Ellington, in his autobiography, said: "Retire to what?" Some keep going, others are forced out by ill health or by changes of musical fashion.

Jess Stacy is a rare exception to the rule. Some fourteen years ago he packed it in; he had had it with music. Jess took a day job in Los Angeles and stayed there until the mandatory retirement age of 65.

The man who, as Benny Goodman's definitive band pianist (class of '39), went on to win several *Down Beat* polls, consolidating his fame in later jobs with Bob Crosby and Tommy Dorsey, today can be found puttering around the garden of his modest, well-manicured home off Laurel Canyon in West Hollywood. Instead of trumpets, trombones and saxophones he is surrounded by grapefruit, lemon and peach trees, all of which he tends constantly. Inside, in the small study with the upright piano, he points to a photograph of a riverboat, framed on the wall: "Look at the crowd on that boat! We were in St. Louis, and that's the SS *St. Paul*, in 1922, the year I played with Tony Catalano's Iowans—and the year my wife Pat was born.

"The only thing I hated about working the boats was playing that steam calliope, with all the cinders from the smokestack and 150 pounds of steam pressure. As we were coming into a town somewhere on the Mississippi, even if it was 5 a.m. I'd have to get up and play the damn calliope to let people know the boat was there."

The career of Jess Alexandria Stacy, born August 4, 1904, in Bird's Point, Missouri, began on the riverboats when he was sixteen and ended in a neighborhood bar one Saturday night early in 1961. "I was only playing two nights a week; I'd already started the day job, walking ten miles a day delivering mail for Max Factor. I was embarrassed by the clientele; the piano was horrible. I thought, who needs this? So I quit."

Big names in jazz die hard. Stacy had to resist the pressure to emerge; finally in 1974 he was persuaded to do a little sound-track work for *The Great Gatsby* and soon afterward was brought to New York to join a parade of pianists at the Newport Jazz Festival. Playing unaccompanied, he stole the show from a half dozen younger men. He stayed in town long enough to make an LP, his first since 1956. (*Stacy Still Swings,* Chiaroscuro CR133).

Another step in the transition from total inactivity to semi-retirement was to be the second Dixieland Jubilee in Sacramento, with Bobby Hackett (who was with Jess on the historic first jam session record for Commodore in 1938) and Teddy Wilson, whose career in the Benny Goodman Trio ran parallel with Jess's years in the Goodman band.

Then back to the peach trees until September and a commitment for a concert in Los Angeles. (They were talking about a European tour for 1976, but the former Patricia Peck, a tall blonde who became the third Mrs. Stacy in 1950, wasn't too sure that this is what either of them would want.)

Stacy looks back on his 40-year career as a time of great

pleasure and little pay: "There were always your Wayne Kings and your Guy Lombardos, the money bands, the icky groups that we wouldn't ever want to play with. In the old days we barely eked out a living—if we made $75 a week that was big money—but we played good dance music; and after the job there would be somebody like Louis to listen to.

"The first band I ever heard that truly amazed me was Fate Marable's on the steamboat *Capitol*. He played good solid dance band piano, and in 1921, when he came to Cape Girardeau he had a kid trumpeter named Louis Armstrong—this was before Louis had been to Chicago or even made any records, and it was like nothing I had heard in my life. That was how you learned in those days—by comparison, by listening. There were no teachers. Bix Beiderbecke taught me in the same informal way. One night in Davenport, in 1924, he sat down at the piano and played the kind of stuff I'd always had in the back of my mind but had never been able to express. He played a song called *Baby Blue Eyes* with the same impressionistic harmony he used years later on *In a Mist*.

Earl Hines I admired; a helluva piano player, but his style wasn't the way I wanted to go. One time I was at the Sunset Cafe in Chicago, hanging around Earl, admiring his work, when Jelly Roll Morton came up to me and said, 'Son, that boy can't play.' Jelly, of course, had a more simplistic style; he didn't get all over the keyboard like Earl."

Stacy's Chicago years, which began in 1925, were summed up briefly: "A band I was traveling with broke up and I couldn't get work, so I had to play for all those gangsters in their speakeasies. They didn't bother yoyu if you stayed sober on the job; but one night at Forest Park, the drummer, George Wettling, got juiced. A mob guy took him out in his car, fired off a tear gas bomb, closed the car door and left George there. Geroge cried for a month.

"Of course, in our off hours we'd all drink and get high. That bootleg gin—you didn't know whether it might be wood alcohol. A lot of people went blind. But down at Taylor and Halstead there was an old Mexican guy who sold weed, and you'd get five sticks for a quarter! Big fat sticks! One night three of us went to his place, and just as we came out with our hands full and started getting into the car, two detectives ran across the street. We threw everything on the floor but it turned out they weren't interested in the grass. They just wanted to know if the old man was selling booze in there. This was before grass became a felony."

Stacy credits his central role in the Goodman orchestra and the Swing Era to the initiatives of John Hammond. "John is the unsung hero. Benny was playing lousy arrangements until John hipped him to Fletcher Henderson, who began to write for the band. Benny was a terrific leader, but I took a lot of guff off him. If I'd had any spunk, instead of being the naive, easygoing young man I was, I'd probably have thrown the piano at him. Still, how could I leave? It was the top band in the country. I didn't get many solos, because Benny featured Teddy Wilson so much; but Teddy and I had a friendly relationship—in my heart I knew he fit better in that trio than I would have. I was more of a band pianist."

Playing in Bob Crosby's band was a relaxing job after four years with Benny. "Bob was easy to work for, but he was always feeling sorry for himself because he had a brother named Bing. And Bob couldn't sing and he knew it. I remember one time he was on 52nd Street and Charlie Barnet was playing. Bob had had a few, and he started to cry. He said 'That man's got talent!' It was pathetic."

Jess was with Tommy Dorsey's band for a few months in 1944-45. Next came a short-lived venture costarring his then wife, singer Lee Wiley, a project he refers to tersely as The Wiley Incident. "She touted me into getting my own band. That was such a rotten band! The class of musicians you could get then were just bums; all the good ones were in the service." After a few more jobs, among them another stint with Benny and a second group of his own, Stacy settled in Los Angeles. "I started playing piano bars. It was all right for a while, but I could see the writing on the wall when TV came in. Some guy at the bar would say: 'Stop playing, we want to listen to the fights.' "

The rest of the 1950s is a hazy montage of bookings that did him less than justice, with a few bright moments interspersed. Charlie Teagarden blowing Bixian horn with Jess at the Hangover. Jack Lemmon playing the warmup music before Jess started the first set at the moribund Garden of Allah, where one of the bungalows had been converted into a bar. Billie Holiday, moribund too, sitting in and singing *Lover Man*. Requests for *Clair de Lune*. For *Down by the Old Mill Stream*. Finally, Stacy says, "I couldn't stand it any more." Before the last measure of his dignity could be stripped from him, his mind was made up.

His quiet and uneventful life now—a life, incidentally, spent on the wagon for many years—suits him fine. He has a son, aged 48, by his first wife, five grandchildren and two great-grandchildren ("one of them is named Jess Stacy"). He likes to recall an incident aboard a steamer not long ago: "My son plays trumpet on the *Admiral* in the summertime. One day the first mate took him aside and said, 'You see that steam calliope? That used to be on the *Capitol*; your daddy used to play it.' " The calliopes, the dismal bars, the endless tours in band buses, the gang-ruled speakeasies today all seem like part of another life, another world. Jess Stacy crosses the living room and sits at the piano. His unique right-hand tremolo makes its way through a Gershwin standard, a blues, a couple of jazz chestnuts. The style, like all the great jazz styles, is aged in the wood; swing era vintage wine.

"Now that you've had a little taste of success with those Newport reviews, don't you have the urge to come back out more regularly?"

"Well," says Stacy, "I will if anybody wants me. That's why I decided to go to Sacramento. They were silly enough to ask me, and I was foolish enough to say yes."

—MAY 1975

BIG BANDSMEN

Thad Jones—Mel Lewis

To Thad Jones and Mel Lewis, the talk about big bands coming back is just so much verbiage. When the Jones/Lewis orchestra came back from its second visit to Japan the trip was so successful that contracts for still another tour were set. In 1973 they came back from an ultra-victorious London visit, where they had laid siege to Ronnie Scott's Club. The year before that, they had come back from the Soviet Union where, under the auspices of the State Department, they had undertaken a five-week sojourn that was acknowledged to have been the most impressive of its kind. It has been one of those bands that was always coming back from somewhere and always in triumph—but never from a tour of the United States.

Jones and Lewis have a uniquely paradoxical track record. They have won polls as the No. 1 big band, yet they never crisscrossed the country in the manner of Kenton, Basie, Herman and others for whom this has been the principal means of survival. They have been an organized unit since 1965, but they have yet to appear on domestic television. (On Easter Sunday, 1972, viewers in the Leningrad and Tallinn areas saw a forty-five-minute Soviet-made Jones/Lewis special.) During a recent Japanese visit, while the emcee introduced each member, the audiences often called out the names beforehand, yet such men as pianist Roland Hanna, trombonist Jimmy Knepper, and the Czech bassist George Mraz remain ciphers to the populace of, say, Detroit or Pittsburgh.

The orchestra has an incomparable consistency in the spirit and cohesiveness of its performance, in the textural and harmonic subtleties of the arrangements by Lewis and others, and in the incredible range of improvisational talent. Every one of the fifteen sidemen is a virtuoso, tied to no special area of jazz, ready and eager to tackle the ensemble's mile-wide scope of moods, tempos and idioms. It is rare also to find a unit in which talent is the only prerequisite, age and race being of no consequence. "We have this brilliant new trumpeter, Jon Faddis, who's twenty, while in the trombone section are Quentin Jackson, who's sixty-five, and Cliff Heather, who's seventy. Nothing matters except that we all have the same attitude about music," Lewis points out.

The band is unique also in its dual captaincy. It is led by Jones, fifty, the brilliant fluegelhornist-composer-arranger, from Pontiac, Michigan, and Lewis, forty-five, the rock-steady Buffalo-born drummer. The two met by chance twenty years before when Jones was playing a gig in Detroit with Count Basie's band and Lewis was working the alternate sets, on the opposite bandstand, with Stan Kenton.

The friendship that developed was an off-and-on affair as their paths crossed only occasionally, but in the early '60s both men settled in New York. For a while they worked together in Gerry Mulligan's orchestra. Also in that band were several others who eventually formed the nucleus of Jones/Lewis when they played their first job at New York's Village Vanguard. At first they seemed like a group of free-lance New York studio musicians finding their aesthetic release from the commercial music world by playing an occasional job with this dream band.

"How," I asked, "have you managed to build from that modest original goal to where you are now?"

"Actually," said Jones, "it was sheer dogged persistence on the part of Mel and me. We felt we had something worthwhile, and in spite of changes in personnel and disappointments along the way, somehow we've managed to survive, and we're determined to keep on keeping on."

Mel Lewis said: "More and more colleges are communicating with one another to line up routes for us. If the University of Iowa wants us to fly out to play for $2,500, it's not viable, but if several other colleges within a 500 to 1,000 mile area can book us during the same week or so, we can afford the transportation, and along the way we can fit in a couple of nightclubs in major cities."

One of the greatest frustrations has been the record situation. The band was under contract to a United Artists subsidiary called Solid State Records, which ceased functioning as an active label in the early '70s. Then came an arrangement with A & M Records, about which Jones and Lewis felt particularly unhappy.

''We were signed for two albums a year. We recorded what we feel was one of our most important pieces, *Suite for Pops,* dedicated to Louis Armstrong,'' Lewis said. ''When we played movements from it during the Russian and Japanese tours, word spread so fast that we were getting requests for it in every city. The reaction was always fantastic. But A & M never released the record.'' (Presumably the firm was too busy pressing up Carpenters albums.)

''Our situation is now very good, though,'' Jones said. ''We've signed as the first jazz artists to record for Philadelphia International.''

How do two bandleaders with possibly conflicting views manage to maintain an equable relationship? Visions of the legendary squabbles between Tommy and Jimmy Dorsey dance through one's head. Jones and Lewis, however, are not blood brothers. They are musical soul brothers. ''And believe it or not,'' says Jones, ''we haven't had a fight in all the years since we met. Isn't that ridiculous?''

Ridiculous or not, it shows up in the musical vibes emanating from the bandstand. Perhaps before long this big band will be coming back, not from Japan or England or Estonia, but from regular coast-to-coast barnstorming, campus-hopping around the country in which the Jones/Lewis dream was born a decade ago. It's about time.

—MAY 1974

(A & M Records released *Suite For Pops* in November 1975, after the orchestra had played it on its second U.S. television show.)

Woody Herman

If you are twelve years old like Tommy Littlefield, you may get an anachronistic, incongruous kick out of singing *Sonny Boy* as a duet with your grandfather in his big, swinging band—especially if your grandfather happens to be Woody Herman.

On the other hand, should you be somewhere in the twenty to thirty zone, the Herman Herd may entice you with the gently rhythmic now-sound of Carole King's *It's Too Late Now* or the wah-wah blandishments of Herbie Hancock's *Fat Mama,* complete with electric piano and fender bass. From there, you may even be able to reach out and relate to the nostalgia-inducing numbers cherished by the over-forties; standards for which there will always be a place in Herman's repertoire—the roaring *Northwest Passage,* the gentle entreaties of Ralph Burns' *Early Autumn* or the saxophonic togetherness of *Four Brothers.*

Woody Herman refuses to accept the suggestion that the great swing bands are good for nothing but nostalgia and, when the handful of surviving veteran leaders dies out, total extinction. "That's the age-old question," he says. "People ask me, 'What's going to happen after you guys are gone?' Well, I'm not worried about the future. It looks brighter than it has since the beginning. In the next five or ten years we're going to hit an era when we'll have our young Artie Shaws, young Duke Ellingtons, young everyone. In other words, they won't need us by then."

He has reached this conclusion through participation in a growing number of college clinics and seminars. The fraternal-order bookings in small towns, once inevitable in the sustaining of a sixteen-man payroll, are gradually giving way to dates played before a younger and hipper audience provided by the schools. "We may have to work two or three times as hard, because we spend the day doing classes with the students, then play a concert at night, but it still beats the world's swingingest Elks Club. I learn as much, playing these dates for the kids, as they learn from us. It's a groove to be involved in such a rewarding avenue of work. I'm only sorry to have gotten into it so late in life: we should have been doing this many years ago."

Many years ago, the Herman personnel included such ambitious youngsters as Neal Hefti, Shorty Rogers, Ralph Burns, Stan Getz, Zoot Sims, Chubby Jackson, Milt Jackson, Terry Gibbs, Oscar Pettiford, Flip Phillips—the list is endless. Not all of them were perfect readers, and back then the only solution was on-the-job training. Today such difficulties barely exist. Almost all Woody's sidemen (most are in their twenties) earned formal college credits in jazz, either at the Berklee College of Music in Boston or among the huge pool of students in the North Texas State University jazz curriculum.

"Our academic system has improved incredibly in the past twenty-five years," Woody said. "Most of the educators now are men who themselves once played in bands like ours; that's why they can communicate so much better than the old line music teacher. Nowadays ninety-nine percent of young people who are seriously into music know the importance of education. They have been indoctrinated in the work of Basie, Kenton, Ellington; they use it as part of their studies. Today the stage bands, which really means jazz bands, number in excess of 35,000 in high schools alone. So everyone who has been touched by this updated approach will become part of a new breed, we will have a whole generation of qualified players, plus an audience of well-trained listeners.''

Herman concedes that media exposure for the big bands still is not what it should be. ''Television has done absolutely nothing for us. Even when you get on a show, you can't be heard properly. TV has moved ahead on many levels technically, but sound quality is right where it was in 1948, with those two-bit speakers. Radio, on the other hand, offers a little more hope. Where the FM and underground stations once used to feed the kids an undiluted diet of heavy acid rock, today the scope is broader; you'll hear some lovely melodic things and some equally heavy jazz along with the rock. Consequently the youth audience is paying attention to the kind of thing bands like mine are doing.''

Some of Woody Herman's earlier attempts to incorporate contemporary material failed, he says, because the arrangers approached their assignments in a condescending or tongue-in-cheek spirit. That was all changed in 1969 with his *Light My Fire* album on Cadet, for which the charts by a black Chicago writer named Richard Evans made the use of pop-rock-soul numbers seem logical and fresh. Since then, with the help of other composer-arrangers such as the young New Zealander Alan Broadbent, who wrote the band's wildly multi-idiomatic fourteen-mintues-long renovation of *Blues in the Night,* the Herman library has expanded into a happy, generation-knitting fusion of then and now sounds. Significantly, the title number of the band's album, *The Raven Speaks,* was composed by Keith Jarrett, an avant garde pianist known for his work with Miles Davis.

Though he always tends to underestimate his personal role, Herman is a stylist at least as distinctive as any of his sidemen. He generates excitement with his climatic solos on clarinet, recalls Johhny Hodges with his serene alto, but reveals a more contemporary personality facet when he picks up his soprano sax. (''John Coltrane's records turned me on to soprano.'') He sings only rarely (''can't learn lyrics,'' he shrugs), but affectingly.

Life on tour in the 1970s has much in common with the one-nighter route of the band's early days. Woody gets to spend an average of twelve weeks a year at home. He and his red-headed Charlotte, a former dancer, have lived since 1946 in a hilltop house overlooking the Sunset Strip. But Charlotte, unlike many band wives, pays her fair share of traveling dues. She recalls that when they celebrated their thirty-sixth anniversary, the Hermans were on the road. "Actually we were in Dallas that day. Woody was preparing for the band's appearance with the symphony." The Dallas initiative was an echo of a venture in 1946, when Herman commissioned Igor Stravinsky to write *Ebony Concerto* for the band's Carnegie Hall debut. For the recent event, Alan Broadbent composed four extended pieces.

"We weren't tied down to any one bag," says Woody. "Alan wrote a mixture of rock, straight-ahead jazz, a waltz, anything that seemed to fit. It took two years to put that whole subject together, but the reaction was so great that we're planning to present it with other symphony orchestras."

While Woody moves onward and upward with the arts, the two generations that follow him have paradoxically headed in the opposite direction. The Hermans' only child, Ingrid, has developed into "one heck of a bluegrass fiddle player," says her father. Ingrid's husband is a bluegrass guitarist from Alabama. Young Tommy, who likes to spend the summers with his grandfather's band (he lives with his parents, who are busy free-lance musicians in Nashville) seems happily steeped in both traditions.

How does a booking agent fill a typical year for a big band in the era of rock combos? There are occasional locations (three weeks in Las Vegas, a fortnight at New York's St. Regis Roof), but for the most part it's a hodgepodge of dance dates, the college concerts-cum-seminars, a little time overseas almost every year (most recently Japan and environs), a few double-decker bookings ("We sold out a 5,000-seat house playing opposite Buddy Rich's band"), and such oddities as a twenty-concert tour in tandem with Shirley Bassey, winding up with a performance at the Los Angeles Music Center.

For a man who, in terms of achievement in his field, has had just about everything, one might expect that the moment had arrived to settle down. But as Charlotte Herman points out: "After all this time he's totally conditioned to that way of life; cars and planes and hotel rooms, and any hall that's ready for the sound of applause." The sound has been ringing in Woodrow Charles Herman's ears since 1936, when he and five other members of the disbanded Isham Jones orchestra formed the basis of a cooperative unit, billed in those early years as "The Band That Plays The Blues." Woody still plays the blues, along with all the other music he has picked up along the way. He emanates pure energy, buttressed by an ensemble of driving, enthusiastic youngsters. For him and for them, the big band spirit is no more obsolescent than apple pie—or even *Apple Honey*.   —JANUARY 1973

Maynard Ferguson

Maynard Ferguson, the Quebec-born trumpeter who has been called leather-lipped and iron-lunged, and who in 1967 quietly, almost mysteriously vanished from the U.S. scene after 18 years as a resident, is back.

Stopping off at Donte's in North Hollywood during a tour of West Coast colleges and clubs, he seemed eager to fill in the gaps. Though his hair is now a ragged mop, his horn stabs with its pristine precision at the out-of-sight, almost out-of-earshot top notes. He talks at the same machine-gun pace, with the same unquenchable fire.

"It began when I went to England supposedly just for one month, with Clark Terry and a few other guys in what they called a 'Top Brass Tour.' By the time the month ended, a lot of English guys had been added and I was fronting a big band at Ronnie Scott's. I guess the fellows thought it odd that a guy on a four-week tour would bring along his wife and five children. And they were all asking 'Where's Maynard and Flo and the kids?' when we didn't show up at the airport; apparently we'd forgotten to tell everyone we weren't going back. This is what probably caused the air of drama, as if we'd disappeared."

Three factors determined his decision. One was discontent with his situation in the States. "I was bored with what I was doing, with what music in general was doing. I'd become some kind of cookie-stamp Maynard Ferguson, and at the time there didn't seem to be any real concern for instrumental music among young people in this country. I also was dissatisfied with the raising of my children."

A second reason was England's immediate attraction for the Fergusons. "During the first tour I played Ernie Garside's club in Manchester. We created an association that's lasted to this day; he's my manager and a good friend. The people in general were hospitable, and the way of life was far less frantic. I formed a big band of north-of-England musicians, to play Ernie's place, in October of '67, and kept it together for the best part of a year. The musicians weren't marvels of technical proficiency, but they loved their job and I worked at their level; we became a great blues band. That was fun, and it allowed me to change my game—which basically was what I was really after."

The third decisive element had to do with Timothy Leary. "That period is dangerous to talk about, because of Tim's current situation, but when I became involved it was all perfectly legal; that was when he was still at Harvard. When Flo and I and the kids moved to the Gatehouse in Millbrook, New York, we were very good friends with Timothy. I was never into anything addicting, though he did get me into the experiments. We didn't see eye to eye on quite a few things; however, you don't have to agree with someone in order to call him one of your best friends, and he is one of my best friends."

Though the Leary episode, Ferguson says, had nothing to do directly with his leaving the United States, it added some confusion to his life. This, along with the breakup of the big band he had led for eight years, and his failure to find new avenues or new audiences, helped constitute reasons for building a new base.

After Manchester came the realization of a long-standing dream. The Fergusons took off for India. "We stayed a year at Rishi Valley School, between Bangalore and Madras in South India, a part of the country that's very beautiful and peaceful. The school, founded on the teachings of Krishnamurti, was a wonderful place for our children." (At the time, in 1968, the younger Fergusons ranged from six to seventeen). "There's a great music and arts faculty; they got into Indian dancing, and studied ancient stringed instruments. I did a little lecturing on Western music and played a few concerts."

Physically and spiritually refreshed, Ferguson returned to the United Kingdom. With a CBS Records contract as an inducement he formed a new big band in London. Two albums, *M.F. Horn* and *M.F. Horn Two*, released in the United States on the Columbia label, sold well enough to trigger the first American tour early in 1972.

Despite the undiminished intensity of his manner, the ex-prodigy, who first came to America direct from five professional years as a teenage wonder, now talks like a man who has found a long-sought inner calm. "The contrast between traveling here and traveling in Europe amazes me. I remember once last year my American agent, Willard Alexander, apologized to me because after three-and-a-half weeks of one-night stands, he had a single night unbooked! Now listen to this. We tour Italy once or twice a year. The jumps are laughable. My guys would be saying, 'Hey, man, we're gonna have to leave at eight to make the gig.' In America that would meean 8 a.m. on the bus to travel all day. In Italy it meant 8 p.m. because the gig was fifteen miles away. Not only that, we'd play four one-nighters and take a couple of days off. Living in England is great, touring Europe is a gas. What I definitely do not want to become is an Ellington, a Basie or a Kenton, in the traveling sense.

"My old friend Willie Maiden, who played sax with me in the '50s and is now with Kenton, said to me when we met last year, 'Isn't it wonderful, man, we finally got to where we can work twelve months out of the year.' Well, it's fine that the audience exists in so many places, but this also can mean 365 gigs. I don't go along with the theory that if a bunch of musicians stay together week after week, year in and year out, they mature and become more excellent. Nonsense. They become more tired, more bored.

"The change is good, the stopping for a while. You need a chance to sit back and think about your music. In England, they let me relax and wait a week after a record date before going in to listen to the playbacks. I've learned things like that by being on the British scene."

He also learned of an encouraging turnaround in the country he left, weary and disillusioned, in 1967. "Our average American fan is now 17 years old. It's all the result of this massive educational program. At a college in Costa Mesa, California. I spent three days, heard some of the forty-three high school and college bands that played there, and found a wonderful renewed awareness. To walk onstage and be known here was a thrill in itself."

He refuses to be trapped into an answer on the permanency of his English home. "After all, the band is international now, so it isn't even true to say we're 'permanently' anywhere. I'm a great believer in destiny and where it's going to put you."

Destiny, which for a while seemed to have placed Maynard in limbo, now seems to have encouraging plans for the mellowed virtuoso.   —MAY 1973

Mercer Ellington

The Duke Ellington orchestra, directed by Mercer Ellington, went to work twenty-four hours after Duke Ellington's funeral. On that day the band flew to Bermuda to fulfill a long-standing commitment. From the moment he inherited the band, Mercer showed a strong sense of awareness of the tremendous responsibility he had taken on. Mercer Kennedy Ellington, heir to the family good looks, the family talent, and now the family orchestra, was the man around whom there circled a great debate: with the loss of its creator, what would beecome of the Ellington legend?

Suddenly, after nine years of relative obscurity as a reticent member of the trumpet section and manager of the band's affairs, the amiable, greatly respected younger Ellington found himself catapulted into a position of prominence he never sought, but must have contemplated at times. His career as a composer and arranger has been all but ignored in the history books, though there was one brief early flurry, when the fight between ASCAP and the networks kept Duke's own music off the air in 1941. The youngster then contributed several illustrious pieces: *Blue Serge, Moon Mist, Jumpin' Punkins* and his best known composition, the blues *Things Ain't What They Used To Be*. But after the initial encouragement, Duke stopped testing his son's talent. Mercer's only showcases were his own short-lived bands or the splinter recording groups led by Johnny Hodges and other Ellingtonians. Why Duke blew hot and cold has remained a mystery.

Mercer Ellington's role would have been more extensive had he remained on hand consistently, but his career in the giant shadow of a genius was marked by fits and starts, the forming and disbanding of several orchestras, the attempts to resolve such problems as inevitably confront a man, no matter how talented, who bears a famous name. Growing up in Washington and New York in the aura of Duke Ellington's regal sounds, he was fascinated and to some extent indoctrinated by his father, who offered him the casual instruction that led to Mercer's first attempts at serious writing. During his teens he had been torn between a career in engineering and the desire to emulate the Old Man. Unlike the senior Ellington, he acquired all the academic advantages: at Columbia, Juilliard and a period of studies of the Schillinger method at New York University. At the age of twenty he led his first band. As a fledgling reporter from *Down Beat*, I gave it a scathing review. Mercer, always the realist, acknowledged my right to criticize the weaknesses of that premature effort. We have been firm friends ever since.

Few realize how much talent came out of the various Mercer Ellington orchestras. In that first unit were Dizzy Gillespie, Calvin Jackson and even Billy Strayhorn, just prior to his affiliation with Duke. After two years in the Army, playing in a band led by Sy Oliver, Mercer tried again. His 1946 band introduced a new singer, a lissome young lady named Carmen McRae. Subsequent orchestras led off and on by Mercer served in effect as incubators to which the senior Ellington turned for some of his personnel. After leading a group at Birdland in New York in 1959, Mercer recorded with an all-star lineup, a mixture of his own and Duke's men. But fate always found him leagues behind, in the undertow.

Between bandleading jobs the search for an identity resulted in a frustrating series of roles. After playing in his father's band for a few months in 1950 he became my partner in a short-lived business venture, Mercer Records, for which we produced several sessions that made us happy if not wealthy; best remembered is the only Duke-and-Strayhorn piano duet album. When this company folded he took a job as a liquor salesman; a year later he was touring with Cootie William's band as trumpeter and road manager; then for several years he worked for his father in a variety of nonplaying functions. Finally, Mercer found a niche that kept him off the road: for three years he was a popular disc jockey on WLIB in New York. But suddenly Ellington Senior beckoned, deciding that he needed someone he could trust as a manager, and that his son might be the ideal trustee. Mercer took the job, along with a seat in the trumpet section, and went back on tour. When his father died he had had enough experience to tackle the gigantic job that confronted him.

The interview below is a composite of a talk I had with Mercer in Bermuda and a telephone conversation a few months later when the band was playing a one-night stand in South Carolina.

FEATHER: Everyone wants to know what's going to happen with the Ellington orchestra.

ELLINGTON: Well, right now we're just trying to get our strength back. We're going to keep things together the best we can, and we hope the band will be as good or better than it has been in years. I want a band that will be able to revive some of the great Ellington works that he stopped playing—things like *Black, Brown and Beige, The Harlem Suite* and *Such Sweet Thunder*, the Shakespeare suite. I have all kinds of ideas I'll be trying to implement.

L.F.: When I spoke to you a few weeks before your father died, you still seemed to be confident that he would be well enough to open with the band in Bermuda. Did you really believe that?

M.E.: Yes. We watched the X-rays until they were almost completely clear and I didn't know what was holding him up. It wasn't until the Monday before he died that we knew it was hopeless. Anyway the whole family went up there; he didn't like to see everyone there at one time and he became very annoyed. He wanted to know what was going on and what we weren't telling him and so forth. But it was just a coincidence that we all happened to get there at the same time.

L.F.: So he never knew it was hopeless?

M.E.: He refused to believe that it was hopeless. He'd been told several times that he was in terrible shape and what the possibilities were, but he refused to believe it wouldn't work.

L.F.: Did he ever discuss with you about your taking over, or what would happen?

M.E.: The closest thing we ever had to a discussion was when we sat together and played the tapes of the Third Sacred Concert, which had been performed at Westminster Abbey. He said: "You know, with good balance, you don't have to go back in the studio." Just that one word "you" was the only hint he gave. Ordinarily he would have said "we." But beyond that, not a word passed between us concerning the possibility of his not coming back.

We were in De Kalb just before we came in off the road the last time, when he went back to the hospital. The guy there said, "Are you going back in immediately . . . or tomorrow?" And he said "What happens if I don't?" The guy said, "I don't see how you can stay out." So Ellington said, "What happens if I do?" "You probably won't come out again." And with that he took off and we made the next date. After that he made just one more date. The day we got to our last date, he just couldn't make it; he turned around and headed back to the airport. That was when these courageous things began to take place, all during that last month. When he was short of breath, when he got up in the morning, you'd swear he could never make it, but he'd get up and be at those concerts that night.

L.F.: Is there any possibility of getting some of the alumni back—

even if only for brief periods?

M.E.: The only problem with that is, who's left?

L.F.: There's Britt Woodman, Cat Anderson . . . several guys on the coast.

M.E.: I've talked to Lawrence Brown about making an occasional guest appearance. That sort of thing would be welcome, but by the same token I feel that Ellington's thinking was justified; some guys were for this particular thing, some for another. As far as the band is concerned, it's a band that should be there always. If you get in the re-cording studio and have one sound, that's the sound that should be with you on the road.

I feel there is a calibre of musician we need to get now that really has to be relative to bringing out the best, including some of the things Ellington felt he couldn't play because this one or that one was missing. We're going to have to figure out what song we're going to play, and then find the musician who can play it. The important thing is that the music of Duke Ellington be authentically represented. It's just like any of the classics—the works of Debussy or Schoenberg, which are continually played as originally conceived. In the same way there are a tremendous number of Ellington's compositions which should never be disturbed from the way they were first presented. Right now, we're almost right back to the original sound of *Mood Indigo*, because in having to readjust, Cootie is playing the melody, with his plunger sound, together with Art Barron and Harold Ashby. That was the group sound the tune had when it was first played.

L.F.: Do you think in due course, when you have time, you might re-sume writing?

M.E.: Yes, in fact I'm working on something right now, and finally getting it rehearsed. For the first time in nine years I'll get to hear something I wrote. One of the first things that came to my mind on the plane over here was to go back and get from someone, somewhere, the original parts to my early compositions. There's a big mass of my material lying around in a basement in one of our buildings. If I can't find them, we'll have to go into the job of transcribing them off the records.

L.F.: The week of Duke's passing must have been really traumatic—the deaths of Paul Gonsalves, Tyree Glenn and your father . . . then all the rehearsals . . .

M.E.: We barely got our breath and went through the motions while we were preparing for Pop's burial . . . rehearsing the band in the morning and going over to the funeral home at night . . . it was good in a way because it kept me busy enough to keep from brooding. You always get the reaction later. You know, after this last European trip we took with the band, there was something in retrospect that I realize . . . certain things happening. Possibly the old man was thinking about these things as his last performances. I know he resented highly a lot of the dates that were booked, all the way to the end of this year, on the premise of farewell performances. He heard about one of them and he exploded, got mad as heck. But his condition deteriorated even more rapidly than the doctors had imagined. From the time he returned from Europe until the month that he played the Rainbow Grill the difference in the size of one of those tumors was just awesome. But Pop kept up a marvelous front. The old man was always a showman.

When he was working on a project, he'd have somebody taking off this part of it, while he had another thing going on this side, and everybody who was only handling a piece of it would wonder how was he ever going to finish it. When he had the whole thing complete, he didn't let the various people know how it all fitted together. I think the people who worked on the A-bomb learned their modus operandi from Duke Ellington! All of a sudden it would all jell right before your eyes. A half hour before the performance of *My People*, he had one part being done in New York and another in Chicago!

L.F.: Would you like to get a pianist who sounds like Duke or would you rather avoid inviting the comparison?

M.E.: The guy I wish was in good enough health to travel with us is Thelonious Monk. But Lloyd Mayers will be a great asset to us. This band is practically new, with nobody to pass the rhythm section information from one to another; and there's no book. The men I need have to not only have a certain ability, they also have to be Duke Ellington fans. That was the great advantage with Joe Benjamin, the bass player. He'd been listening to Ellington records for years. When he came to a certain number, he'd remember what Blanton had done on it.

A lot of the cats I think I'm looking for are not in New York. They're somewhere between the West Coast, Texas and Kansas City. There's less competition in those areas and the guys out there don't have the kind of work that we can give them. We can offer each other something that we're both not getting right now.

There are two bands I had that I'll never forget: the one I had that went into Birdland for two weeks; and the ten-piece group we used in Las Vegas. This band, just as it is, could jell. But if it doesn't there are certain things that I feel we have to do in order to maintain the Ellington prestige. We have to have certain people in certain places, just as in the early days we had people like Clark Terry, Cat, Tricky, Lawrence Brown—all the fellows Duke wrote for with their specific sound in mind.

I think we can do it, and that's what I'm going to be working on between now and the time when the band will really be back in action, full steam ahead. I want to have a band that Pop would be proud of. I think I can make it.   —OCTOBER 1974

Buddy De Franco

On two recent nights in Birmingham, Alabama, the Glenn Miller orchestra had two conductors: Buddy De Franco, who had led the band for eight years, and, overlapping with him on those transitional evenings, Michael (Peanuts) Hucko, who had taken over the care and feeding of the indestructible ghost, leaving De Franco free to resume his career as a jazz clarinetist.

Despite the inevitable monotony, those years of bringing *In The Mood, A String Of Pearls* and *Chattanooga Choo Choo* to every corner of the globe were financially stable and not without their musical rewards, De Franco says. "Those old Miller arrangements may sound easy, but they play hard. We had guys in the band who had worked with Buddy Rich, Kenton and Herman, and even they had trouble reading the parts correctly. However, Buddy Rich at one time or another took twelve guys from our band! The name of Glenn's game was precision and self-discipline. Younger players today tend to be too loose at times, so the Miller music still offers valuable experience."

All through the years of De Franco's adsence from jazz clubs and festivals, he never lost touch with the fans who had voted him No. 1 clarinetist in the *Down Beat* poll every year from 1945-54, and then off and on until 1967. Moving back into an essentially different world, he nevertheless felt that his eminence would quickly be regained. "In fact," he said, "I picked up a lot of followers along the way. During the Miller dates I did play some jazz, especially at concerts. People came in to hear us who used to listen to my jazz group. They're pretty loyal—especially in Japan and Europe, where I couldn't get off the stage without playing some jazz. They demanded it!"

The new schedule was found to be far easier on De Franco than the endless round of one-nighters for an organization controlled by administrators of the Miller estate. "I'll never again go out for more than two or three months at a time. I've bought a home in Panama City, Florida, and from there I'll take out a jazz combo to play campus clinics, where there's still a lot of interest in me; also some jazz clubs and festivals, possibly including Newport and Monterey; and of course overseas tours. I feel I have something to say to today's jazz audience, and I want to seize the opportunity before it's too late."

To help the restoration process, De Franco recorded a quintet album with Roland Hanna, piano; John Chiudini, guitar; George Mraz, bass and Mel Lewis, drums. The record was to be distributed by mail order, with Mraz and Hanna, both regular members of the Thad Jones-Mel Lewis band, going out on gigs with De Franco when their schedules permitted.

In retrospect, the years as leader of a band so far removed from his original musical values were only tiresome when the requests for the obvious big ones came up. "We'd even have these self-appointed authorities asking for tunes Glenn didn't launch. Like one night a woman said that I'd missed the famous Glenn Miller hit, *Opus One*. I said, 'That wasn't Glenn Miller, that was Tommy Dorsey.' She replied, 'Oh, no, young man, I have all the records.' I had to tell her, 'Don't "young man" me—I was on that record with Dorsey!'

"It was a pleasure to do the better Miller things, though, like Bill Finegan's arrangements of *Serenade In Blue*, *I'm Old Fashioned* and *Skylark*, and the Billy May-Finegan *Volga Boatmen*. Those never became a bore to play."

Peanuts Hucko, who worked for Miller's 1943-44 AAF band in England and France, is a clarinetist whose jazz credentials are almost as impressive as De Franco's. After making the big band route with Will Bradley, Ray McKinley and briefly on sax with Benny Goodman, he worked for several years at Eddie Condon's Club, put in time with Louis Armstrong and Jack Teagarden, and—handily, in view of the Miller band's frequent trips to Nippon—became a big man during extensive tours of the Far East; his record of *Suzukake no Michi* with Shoji Suzuki's Rhythm Aces was a top seller on RCA-Japan during the 1960s.

In recent years Hucko has lived in California, where he served (1970-72) as featured soloist on Lawrence Welk's TV show. Compared with the Welk experience, his Miller travels were bound to find him somewhat less remote from his kind of people. Moreover, he has been given by the Miller office what might be characterized as quart-blanche: "About 25% of the arrangements can be anything I want. So I'm taking some of my own music along, and will have new material written that's less traditional than the Miller style."

Thus to the ongoing legend of the most popular orchestra in musical history there was added still another bandleader. After Glenn's death Tex Beneke was the first on tour under the Miller banner; Ray McKinley led a Miller band from 1956 until January of '66 when De Franco took over.

Jazz has undergone so many radical changes that it will be intriguing to see how well today's public responds to De Franco. As he has said, there is little competition for him in his field; the clarinet has been a neglected instrument in jazz, spawning no completely qualified new-comers, no inspired or inspiring future stars, since De Franco himself left the scene. With luck and careful management this singularly gifted musician should have a good chance of being able to pick up just where he left off, too many years ago.   —FEBRUARY 1974

(In September of 1974 Peanuts Hucko, on the verge of physical exhaustion, quit the Miller orchestra. "How Buddy took it for eight years beats me," he said. "It was as much as I could take to handle it for eight months.")

Bob Crosby

"When I've got a real great band behind me," says Bob Crosby, "I never try to do much singing. Even if I wanted to, I probably couldn't, because I had it scared out of me many years ago."

The public image of George Robert Crosby has always been slightly blurred. This can be attributed partly to the years spent in the shadow of an elder brother who was the best-known male singer in the world; and to the paradox of his role as the only major bandleader of the swing era who conducted a lot, sang a little, and didn't play an instrument at all.

In the nostalgic swing band revival, bookings are coming in more readily for his full orchestra. He had been out of the big band business for some fifteen years until Disneyland lured him back. In the interim he played a variety of roles as television emcee (he spent a year in Australia hosting a *Tonight*-type show), failed businessman ("I went into the car rental business in Hawaii, managed to lose $75,000 and go broke in eight months") and small combo leader. His original big band years were 1935-42. During that time he also introduced an eight-piece band-within-the-band, known as the Bob Cats. Since about 1955 he has fronted various reincarnations of this smaller group, often reuniting several of the original members.

Today Crosby no longer has any professional sibling traumas to battle. The gray hair is mostly white now; a distinguished looking six-footer, his 185 pounds in good shape, he has lived for several years in the conservative community of La Jolla, near San Diego. He and his attractive blonde wife June have three sons, two daughters and five granddaughters. (Mrs. Crosby, a cooking expert, writes food columns for various magazines). "On September 27," Crosby said gently, "I'm going to award her the Victoria Cross and the Purple Heart. On that day she will have put up with me for thirty-three years."

When he is not out of town playing a band gig, Crosby may be in the studios taping one of his three-a-month commercials for a savings and loan company or attending a meeting of the local Mental Health Association, with which he has been intensely active. "It's not a popular disease—cancer is easy to raise money for, but people tend to relate mental health to straitjackets."

His roller-coaster career began, like his brother's, when he came out of Gonzaga University into show business. The youngest of seven children and nine years Bing's junior, he went directly from college to the Anson Weeks orchestra.

"I did pretty well when I was with Anson," he said in a rare moment of favorable self-appraisal. "Then Tommy Rockwell, the booking agent, came to hear me. He said: 'We're organizing a new band with the Dorsey Brothers, and I'm going to put you with them.' Although I liked their records and enjoyed Jimmy Dorsey's sax work, I was reluctant. Tommy Dorsey, in my opinion, was never a great jazz trombonist. Anyhow, I joined the band at the Sands Point Bath Club in Great Neck, Long Island, New York.

"Those opening nights are burned in my mind like a nightmare. The first two nights nobody spoke a word to me; I didn't sing a single note, just sat at a table. The beginning of the third night, Tommy Dorsey came over to me and in his very tender way said, 'Look, this is the best band in the whole world, and you ain't the best Crosby singer. I didn't want you in this band. Rockwell put you here. I'm not going to have any arrangements written for you. If you find something in the library that you can sing, walk up there and sing it. If you can't, tough.'"

Crosby managed to live through a grueling year with the unsentimental gentleman. "It got worse when a theater in Baltimore used the billing 'Bing Crosby's Brother, Bob, with the Dorsey Brothers Orch.' Tommy flipped, and of course we made them change it. Soon after that Gil Rodin, a saxophonist, offered me a job of fronting a band he'd formed out of the nucleus of the defunct Ben Pollack orchestra. By that time Tommy was glad to get rid of me, and since I was only making $75 a week I figured it was time for a change."

The experience with Dorsey, says Crosby, robbed him of any self-confidence he might have acquired as a singer and "left me with a nervous vibrato that I've never been able to get rid of." His anxieties were aggravated by the "Bing's Brother" syndrome.

Recently he was approached to write an autobiography. "How can I tackle it without sounding bitter? Which I'm not. I'd have to tell some rather weird things about the enigma whom I love as a brother, but whom I find very strange."

"Strange in what way?"

"Well, for example, he has no friends."

Having done his share of psychoanalyzing over the years, Crosby elaborated: "Coming from a poor background, when Bing had his first huge success he was so frightened that he built a sort of big cellophane bag around himself. He lives in this bag and opens it now and then for a little while. You can only get inside for a minute; then he shuts you out.

He's done so many wonderful things, and some others that I just can't understand, it's a peculiar feeling to have some friend walk up and say to you: 'I guess you had your brother over for dinner last night. Saw him arriving at the airport.' But the truth is that although he's passed through San Diego many times, he hasn't called me in three or four years, so all I can ever say to these friends is 'No.' Because Bing is adored to such a tremendous degree, they'll figure, well, if he didn't call me, I must be the one who did something wrong. This hardly helps my standing in the community.

"Bing is one of the most sentimental men I've ever known, and he's scared stiff of showing this sentimentality. He doesn't want anyone to get close enough to see it. The only real buddy-buddy friend he had was Eddie Lang."

I did some mental arithmetic: Lang, the guitarist in Paul Whiteman's orchestra when Bing was its vocalist, died in 1933. If Bob's estimate is correct, Bing has been without a true friend for about four decades.

Bing was not involved with the launching of the Crosby orchestra, which turned out to be the first event in Bob's career to earn him a measure of identity. Great soloists emerged from the Crosby band as they had from Goodman's and Shaw's. Many of them continued to work with Crosby off and on for decades after the band broke up. Matty Matlock on clarinet, Nappy Lamare on guitar, saxophonist Deane Kincaide and trumpeter Zeke Zarchy, all members of the band in the 30s, all have been back with their old boss.

Crosby is characteristically self-denigrating in assessing his role as a leader. "Originally, as Bing's brother, standing in front of a jazz band, I felt this was not quite the ideal image for the guys, and I'm still sure the band would have gained stature if Jack Teagarden or someone of that caliber had been the leader.

"I did play one important part. I was able to introduce the sidemen in a conversational way that helped sell their music. It's the same in any of the arts. I can see a painting and not be impressed; then I may meet the artist, go back and see the painting again and understand it. Well, I could stand between Eddie Miller and our audience and make what he was about to say on his horn comprehensible to the people. That was the only talent I had. If I'd stood up there and sung ballads all night it would have been a drag for the crowd who wanted to hear those great guys playing. As for the musicians themselves—well, if I'd done a long, slow love song, Ray Bauduc would have just fixed his drums very loudly through the whole number.''

Crosby underestimates himself. He had then, and still has, a certain charisma that makes him at once more than a singer and more than a go-between for his sidemen. Coupled with this quality is a deep and abiding love for the kind of music with which he came to be associated. Though he finds it difficult to express in words, he came closest when asked about his plans for the future.

''I'll still play dates with the big band whenever I can get them. We've played at conventions of teamsters, construction workers, automobile manufacturers. Those are the only kinds of dates that can pay enough money for me to hire the kind of men I want.

''After all these years, though, there's still no greater feeling than standing in front of a great swinging orchestra and hearing those beautiful arrangements unwind. My job has involved so many things the audience doesn't know about. All of us were so close, we lived like a family. Being a bandleader is trying to get a baby sitter for a trumpet player so his wife can come to the gig, otherwise she'll give him hell and he won't be in the mood to play. It's helping the trombonist find his lost suitcase, and advising the pianist on whether to get a divorce. Sure I'd like to write an honest book about the Crosbys, but it wouldn't be complete unless I wrote about my other family, too.''

—AUGUST 1971

VOICES

Sarah Vaughan

"She is not merely a vocalist, but a brilliant, interpretative musician able to improvise, leave her audience breathless with her fantastic versatility, whether in person or via her many recordings"—the kind of words to which Sarah Vaughan has become accustomed over the years. But the speaker, the occasion and the place added a touch of distinction; Representative Thomas M. Rees (Democrat of California) included them in a 500-word speech in the House of Representatives saluting Sarah Vaughan on her fiftieth birthday.

It's been a winding road, often unpaved, from the Apollo Theatre in Harlem, with occasional snippets in the jazz magazines as the only markers, to birthday proclamations from Mayor Bradley and Governor Reagan, capped by a glowing review in the Congressional Record. A long jump, too, from the shy, skinny, Newark, New Jersey girl with the gapped front teeth and the introverted manner, and from the passive, permissive wife of two stormy marriages ("Christ, if I had to do my life over, those are the two things I'd do without") to the cheerful, attractive, outgoing Vaughan of today, with two and a half acres of rolling countryside at the Hidden Hills home she shares with her daughter Debbie, her mother, a sister, and Marshall Fisher, the friendly, non-aggressive man who, in the view of all who know Sassy, has been largely responsible for her peace of mind.

Ms. Vaughan and Fisher returned recently from a gig she said was one of the most unorthodox and rewarding of her career. "I was in Lesotho—that's the former British protectorate of Basutoland. Since 1966 it's been an independent black nation, but it's a totally encircled enclave, so we had to stop in Johannesburg and wait two hours for a train to take us there. There was a little incident, which wound up with a Jewish lady helping me out and then saying 'I shouldn't kiss you 'cause I might get in trouble,' but she kissed me anyway. Sing in South Africa? God, no. I wouldn't spend another minute there if they gave me 10 million in cold cash.''

In Maseru, the capital of Lesotho, the unifying power of music was telling. ''Once they're out of South Africa, the people are so different. Some of them chartered buses and traveled up to 1,000 miles; every night there were people who'd come from as far as Capetown. The money was good, and I worked in a big hall, with a casino jammed with high-rollers.'' The Maseru audience, where Sarah found ''the happiest people I've ever seen,'' is among her most pleasant remembrances. Asked where else she had found heartwarming receptions, she replied without a moment's pause: ''Rio. They just love beautiful music in Brazil. Rotterdam is fantastic—I was in the dressing room changing to go home, then had to go back out—and found half the audience onstage, almost crushing me. The opera house in Venice was the most beautiful place I ever worked. I thought I was—let's see, who did I think I was? An opera singer?''

When I remarked that her range, timbre and musicianship qualify her for operatic roles, and wondered whether she had ever had ambitions along those lines, she said: ''Yes, I always wanted to; but you have to start early, and I couldn't afford the money for lessons. I was thrilled once to receive a telegram of congratulations from Marian Anderson, and flattered when Zubin Mehta said it was his loss and popular music's gain; but I think I'm happier where I am. After all, opera you can be taught; but what I do I have to feel, which I believe is better.''

She was around nineteen and working as vocalist with the Billy Eckstine orchestra, when Dizzy Gillespie, then a trumpeter in that band coaxed me into a studio to hear a demo he had made with Sarah. I was convinced that the sound was like no other vocal jazz, but was rebuffed by several record firms before one company grudgingly set up the terms for what became, on New Year's Eve of 1944, the first Sarah Vaughan record date: $20. for each of her four vocals, and $12.50 per tune for my services as producer. During the next few years she made a series of 78s that left her contemporaries incredulous. Nor were they all jazz-oriented. She introduced *Tenderly,* launching it as one of the most enduring of pop standard ballads; and her version of *The Lord's Prayer* lives in some memories as the most consummately beautiful treatment of that song; but along with most of her masterpieces it has long been unavailable. Her soaring contralto has graced hundreds of performances, but her only major hit was in 1959—a forgettable ditty called *Broken Hearted Melody* for which, with a gulp, she still takes requests. "Why can't I be stuck" she said, "with a song like *What Are You Doing The Rest Of Your Life*?"

She was off the record scene entirely for five years until Bob Shad, an old friend who had produced for her at Mercury in the 1950s, invited her to join his Mainstream label. Her best-known album during this alliance has been a set of Michel Legrand songs, with the composer conducting and arranging. "Over the years, though, I've recorded some pretty bad songs, trying to get a hit, and they keep haunting me. It's nice to have a hit, but I'm lucky; I don't need it. Billy Eckstine and I have a lot in common; he always works and does very well, with or without a big record. To be a legend is what keeps you going. When I was completely off the record for those four or five years, that's when I realized I must be a legend, too. It sure is a nice feeling to know that people will remember you after you're gone—that you'll manage to be a little bit of history."   —APRIL 1974

Cleo Laine

The *London Sunday Times,* not normally given to hyperbole, called her "quite simply the best singer in the world." The statement was in a sense incomplete, since it made no mention of Cleo Laine's innumerable credits as an actress—in straight drama, musical comedy, opera and revues. Looking through a thick wad of clippings reviewing her concerts, records, plays, you would swear they were all written by her publicist. From *Time* and *Newsweek* to the *Los Angeles Free Press,* the superlatives are unanimous. In England her record sales topped the million mark as far back as 1961.

Then why is it, one might ask, that if you mention her name to ten people in the average American city you find that 9.99 of them have never heard of her? Two simple answers: lack of exposure on major record labels, insufficient time spent in this country. Too busy being a smash at festivals in Great Britian, Australia, across Europe, behind the Iron Curtain. One night in 1959, when her husband John Dankworth was leading his big band at Birdland, she sat in for a couple of numbers; but the first official Laine-Dankworth U.S. appearance was a concert at New York's Alice Tully Hall in the fall of '72.

"Part of our problem," says Dankworth, "has been that we have no backlog here. No people in our age bracket can say, as they do in England, 'I remember you from back in my college days.' We're almost starting from scratch." But, as Cleo hastened to add, "The people here were incredible. At the Rainbow Grill in New York Burt Bacharach, Lena Horne, Tony Bennett, Cy Coleman, Benny Goodman and Schuyler Chapin, general director of the Metropolitan Opera, all came to see us. Then we did our second Carnegie concert and RCA recorded it—our first live album in the States." A Cleo cult proliferated so swiftly in New York that, as Dankworth remarked, "She can't go anywhere without being recognized on the street." (New York is not your average American city.) "I've been offered two or three musicals, one by Michel Legrand," said Cleo, "but that's a tricky step in an American career. In England shows usually run long enough to try to prove themselves; on Broadway you can become a star overnight or close right after you open if the critics don't like you."

On this, their third collaborative American visit, the Dankworths finally took the plunge in the form of a cross-country tour. "We expected to play a lot of empty halls," John admitted, "but it hasn't been that way at all. Good attendance everywhere." Cleo, whose speaking voice is a deep, sonorous counterpart of her singing contralto, said: "American audiences show their feelings a lot more. Of course, it's an established fact that the British personality is less demonstrative. English people have kept me in their hearts, though, and I know they're appreciative, but my goodness, at Carnegie Hall they actually threw flowers at me!" The awe with which Cleo Laine is regarded by her peers can be ascribed to an astronomical range, a smoky, aged-in-the-wood sound, the total experience effect of her jazz-pop-Shakespeare-Bessie Smith-Dickens-rock-W. H. Auden repertoire, and the unique chemistry of her fusion with John Dankworth in his roles as saxophonist, clarinetist, composer, arranger and conductor.

Their lives first converged in 1952, when she joined Dankworth's septet at seven quid a week in a small club off Charing Cross Road. Cleo was born Clementine Dinah Campbell in Southall, Middlesex, October 27, 1927. (At the time, Dankworth was a five-weeks-old wailer in Walthamstow, Essex.) Cleo's English mother was disowned by her parents for marrying a West Indian. (As one observer has said, "If all mixed marriages could produce offspring like Cleo, they should be obligatory.")

She made her debut at three, warbling *Let's All Sing the Barmaid's Song* at a community variety show. Despite extensive study of piano, violin and dancing, her late teens were spent in frustrating odd jobs: hairdresser, milliner, pawnshop clerk, cobbler, librarian. Raised on the records of Billie, Ella, Sarah, Cleo was well suited to the values of the Dankworth group. John, who spent some of his formative days as a musician aboard the Queen Mary, was able through those transatlantic trips to absorb the wonders of 52nd Street jazz, particularly of Charlie Parker. After Cleo had worked for a year with the combo, Dankworth organized a big, swinging jazz orchestra. By 1958, the year of their marriage, she was dividing her time between his band and the legitimate theatre. ("I didn't get much work at first, because I was typecast as a black actress; but that soon changed.") She was Titania in a West End production of *A Midsummer Night's Dream*; doubled as Ellen Terry and Mrs. Patrick Campbell in a musical on the life of George Bernard Shaw; played Hedda Gabler at Canterbury; replaced Lotte Lenya in the Brecht-Weill opera *The Seven Deadly Sins*. Through the 1960s a series of recording ventures produced such gems as *Shakespeare and All That Jazz* (sonnets sung by Cleo Laine; music by John Dankworth, words by William Shakespeare). As a climactic touch, Cleo Laine rattled off the titles of all the Bard's plays to a charming melody in *The Compleat Works*. Time: one minute twenty-three seconds. Love's labour well invested.

John Dankworth has had a multiple career of his own. From a modest start in the late '40s playing Dixieland with Freddie Mirfield's Garbage Men, he worked his way up to victories in the *Melody Maker* poll. A Fellow of the Royal Academy of Music, he too has crossed all the borderlines, working with symphony orchestra, composing a string quartet and a piano concerto, making his bow in film scoring with the award-winning *We Are The Lambeth Boys*, followed by *Saturday Night and Sunday Morning*, *The Servant*, *Darling*, *Morgan*, *The Idol* and *The Engagement* among others.

He has conquered the world of television music (notably with his *What The Dickens* orchestral suite, which won an Ivor Novello award, and in the prestigious series *Survival*), and found lucrative success in commercial jingle writing. Meanwhile, in July of 1971, Cleo's consummate artistry led to her greatest triumph, as Julie in a London revival of *Show Boat*. Except for leaves of absence to tour with John in concerts, she stayed in the show, earning nightly standing ovations, until it closed.

The Dankworths since 1967 have been living with their children, Alexander and Jacqueline, at the Old Rectory, built around 1860 on seventeen acres of land in Buckinghamshire. There they have constructed a 200-seat theatre and set up their Wavenden Allmusic Plan, a charitable non-profit organization that has succeeded in breaking down musical barriers. There are year-round courses for children, and regular concerts. Julie Felix, Rolf Harris, the Alberni String Quartet, Dudley Moore, the Northern Sinfonia, Andre Previn, Larry Adler and Ronnie Scott have performed at Wavenden.

How much time they will be able to spend at home in the coming years is unpredictable. The astonishing success of their first serious attempt to break into the American market has prompted them to appear in the United States for considerably longer periods.

Cleo Laine and John Dankworth, panidiomatic products of more than two decades in every region of the musical arts, number, among their diverse fans, Galt McDermott (whose *African Waltz* John was the first to record in 1960), Miles Davis and Princess Margaret. The only world they have yet to conquer completely—American show business at large—seems to be theirs for the asking.   —NOVEMBER 1973

Mahalia Jackson

Mahalia Jackson flopped down on the living room couch in her Los Angeles home, one of sixteen apartments in a building she owns. "Ten years ago," she said, "I took what little bit the good Lord gave me, and put it down on some property. I still really live in Chicago, but I'm blessed to have a home out here. Child, I'm so glad to be back, I could cry. I was in the air so long—I'm too old for all that stuff. Right now, I'm so tired, I'm sick."

"All that stuff" was a tour, the first in her fifty-nine years, that took her to Japan for three weeks and to India for twelve days. From the first moment off the plane in Tokyo, a wave of adulation swept her along that could have been likened only to the second coming of the Beatles. "I never was treated so royally in my life," said America's most renowned bearer of the gospel. "Nothing but the elites to meet me everywhere. They just about had me eating myself to death at banquets and official lunches and everything. I left here wearing a size 18, and now look at me—I can just about get into a size 22.

"Everywhere I went, I found people giving praises to the Lord. Gospel is universal. Do you know what I saw in my hotel room? A group of Japanese gospel singers imitating our great Christian songs on television, in perfect English." In her hegira, several gaps were bridged: those of generation, nationality, race, and no less significantly, religion. A press conference in Tokyo was held in a ballroom packed with 200 representatives of all the media, religious publications among them.

"Their questions didn't bother me; I told them why I had such faith in my God, but I didn't want to convert anyone or deny that Buddha was a prophet, a foreteller before Christ. At the first concert they had someone translating my songs. I'd be standing up there breathing between lines, and the Reverend Joseph Love would walk up—he's a Jesuit priest from Boston who's on the faculty at Sophia University in Tokyo—he'd tell them what I'd been singing about. But between the Americans in the audience and the Japanese who understood English, or those who just got the message from the way I sounded, he didn't need to do that. The rest of the places, there was no interpreter—I just sang. The people went so wild until one time I had to do four concerts in one day, and sold out every house."

The performance that will remain longest in her memory played to a much smaller audience. It was agreed that she should give a concert for Emperor Hirohito at the Imperial Palace in celebration of his 70th birthday. The emperor was called away at the last minute, but the concert was staged before the empress, other members of the royal family and a few friends. The only Westerners invited were United States Ambassador Armin Meyer and his wife. (Meyer told friends that Miss Jackson's appearance had gained him his first social invitation to the palace in his two years on the job.)

One song that left a special impression was *Who Made the Great Plan?* Its rhythmic, blues-tinged, testifying story toppled centuries of tradition and protocol as royal heads nodded to the beat and feet tapped in rhythm. A scroll bearing the lyrics was later handed to the emperor, along with a tape of the concert. After the performance, the empress invited the singer to a private conference (an almost unheard of honor for a Westerner, especially an entertainer) and presented her with a 600-year-old vase.

Lorraine Goreau, composer of *Who Made the Great Plan?* tagged along with Miss Jackson. "Everywhere we went in Japan," she recalls, "the emotional reaction was devastating. On the up tempo tunes Mahalia had them shouting *Hallelujah,* and you'd have sworn she was back home in New Orleans. On some of the more solemn numbers you could see tears streaming down their faces."

The Indian segment of the tour was sponsored by the State Department. Accordingly, in addition to the scheduled concerts there was a continuous round of official receptions, dinners with public affairs officers, a party tendered by Ambassador Kenneth Keating and, to the amazement of everyone who had set up the schedule, an unplanned backstage summit meeting with (and at the special request of) Prime Minister Indira Gandhi. In Calcutta and New Delhi every seat was sold out less than two hours after they were placed on sale. Madras and Bombay were not far behind.

"We played at St. Thomas, a 500-year-old cathedral in Bombay. It was the only place in town that had an organ." (Miss Jackson was accompanied throughout the tour by Charles Cleveland Clency, her organist, and Gwendolyn Lightner at the piano.) "The pastor got up and told the people not to appluad. They were mad, but I thought it was correct; I had to tell them this was the principle of the church, and that the churches are not built to entertain, but to revive."

In New Delhi, government officials had briefed Mahalia on the impending presence of the prime minister. "They told me she would just stay while I did three numbers; then she'd leave, and after an intermission I'd do the rest of the concert. At the intermission, instead of leaving, she asked Ambassador Keating to bring her backstage to meet me. Some folks had told me she is a very strong and temperamental woman, but that wasn't the way I found her. She's a woman who's very careful with her words, and she talks quite slow. She said to me: 'Your music comes straight from the soul. Your concert was wonderful.' Then she smiled, which is another thing people say she doesn't do. And she spoke warmly about my beloved Dr. Martin Luther King. When I went back out to sing for the people, Mme. Gandhi was walking out the front entrance; but when she heard the piano and then my voice, she turned right around and came back to hear the entire concert. For a while she was just standing there under a fire exit sign until somebody offered her a seat. While all this was going on, the security guards like to went crazy."

Repertoire during the Indian concerts was partially governed by the familiarity of some members of the audience with Miss Jackson's recordings. "Most of the songs they asked for were off the old, old records, from the days when I was recording 78s for the Apollo label back in New York. Those records are still selling over there. At a memorial concert for Whitney Young, which was staged in a cathedral in Bombay, I sang *Be Still My Soul* and *Going Home*. But I often deviated from the program completely—I'm always doing that. One time I felt so grateful that the Lord had given me strength to go through with this tour in spite of my heart condition—I had an attack in 1964, you know—that I just fell into singing one of them great old songs, something I don't think I'd sung in thirty years, called *I Woke Up This Morning With My Mind Stayed on Jesus*. I sang it *a cappella*. That really did it with the people."

After twenty-five years as an international symbol of black American society, Mahalia remains unshaken in her simple optimism. She is given to remarks like: "Mayor Daley sees to it that the U.S. Embassy meets me everywhere I go. He knows that I represent America. It's my home. The older generation only acted according to what they could see and understand in their day. Young people are seeing better than the older folk; they got more knowledge, they're wise enough to see through all the hypocrisy. Sure, you still find a few people cliquing together, but in time things are going to reach a peak, where all people will want to be free. I have a chance, more than the average black to meet all kinds of people, to see and talk about the happier side of things. I can see a brighter day coming and a better understanding among and between all races.''

It is not difficult to understand why the State Department sees a perfect ambassador of good will in the queen of gospel. If her booking office has its way it will not be long before she is off again, bringing her message to the European audiences who have been taking her into their hearts since her first foreign tour in 1952.

"Them agents want me to go over there for eight weeks. I don't want to go, but then again, there's something about this work that just possesses you. All of us gotta die sooner or later, and as long as I love what I'm doing, that's the way I want it. I know I'm going to go some day on that stage but I don't care. I'm grateful to the Lord for what I've had.'' —JUNE 1971

(Mahalia Jackson died January 27, 1972 of heart failure—not onstage, but at the Little Company of Mary Hospital, Evergreen Park, Illinois. She was sixty years old.)

Clara Ward

While contemporary jazz has widened its access in recent years to churches and synagogues of the Western world, a form of melodic-poetic justice has completed the cycle. Such temporal arenas as supper clubs, jazz festivals and Nevada casinos have come to play host to the reverential songs of the likes of Clara Ward.

There is no other chronicle quite like that of the Ward singers. More than any other such group, they have succeeded in demonstrating the universality of the Negro gospel song, the degree to which its participants can diversify their repertoire, the relationship of gospel and its younger cousin, jazz, and the ability of this vibrant idiom to transcend religious and racial lines.

Miss Ward, a small, poised woman who carries her 43 years lightly, despite a voluminous wig that contrives, during offstage hours, to lap down in disarray over her shoulders and part of her handsome face, speaks in smooth, evenly modulated tones that contrast strikingly with the bristling energy of that same voice lifted in song. How, I wondered, was the transition from a strictly religious context to the secular world accomplished? When did the Wards turn in their long choir robes for the rich silks and brocades that became their official regalia? "It all happened gradually," said Miss Ward. "My mother, Gertrude Ward, wants me to have all the credit now, but she had the first group of female gospel singers and started the whole movement that made gospel what it is today. When I was nine years old, we started as a trio—my mother and my sister and me. We enlarged a few years later. The group played the Negro church circuit. In 1947 John Hammond, the man who discovered Billie Holiday, got hold of my first solo record and wrote me up in a white newspaper. It was the first time I'd ever seen my picture in print."

Still the singers remained in the black communities across the country, wearing out fifteen of their specially built eight-door limousines as they traveled from ghetto to ghetto. They sang at a theater in 1955, the Apollo in Harlem, but the first sign of a breakthrough to the general public came in 1957 with an invitation to the Newport Jazz Festival, as part of an all-gospel matinee. "Two years later, we made our first European tour. Then in 1961 we played our first club booking, at the Village Vanguard in New York." By now the religious sextet had become a full-bloomed visual act, with matching gowns and trademark coiffures. In 1962 Miss Ward, whose mother had quit when the girls began to work the nightclubs, took her troupe into Disneyland, where they appeared every summer thereafter. "While we were there, a talent scout from Los Angeles caught us. He offered us a two-week booking. We took just enough clothes for two weeks, but we wound up staying for forty weeks straight, in 1963. Same thing again in '64. We felt at home; we could walk up and down the aisles just like we do in church. We loved it."

Why did the square Nevada audience, with its high percentage of elderly white conservatives, Texas oilmen and the like, react so receptively to Negro gospel music? "Don't forget," Miss Ward remonstrated, "Southerners know plenty about church music—even white southerners. They go to a lot of colored churches; we used to sing down South at churches where everybody brought along people that they worked for. Besides, in their own churches they sing a lot of our songs too." Miss Ward spoke of the segregated church system as if it were a fact of life to be taken in stride. She was no less pragmatic in an analysis of her system for programming shows. "During the first show at Las Vegas, we do what you would call the square material; but as the night goes by, we start putting in real church songs, and by the time the last show comes around, especially when we have people in the audience that understand—people like Steve Lawrence, Eydie Gorme, Dean Martin—we sing a complete church program."

(Dean Martin?)

In these times of social turbulence, since so many black and white youths have expressed disillusionment with the church, it would seem that a concomitant decline in the interest in religious music might be imminent, especially among militants. When this sensitive topic was broached, Miss Ward demurred: "So far, I haven't met that crowd. Maybe I'm just lucky, but all the people at the churches I go to react just the way they did twenty or thirty years ago."

Even among rebellious college audiences, she added, there seemed to be no pressure. "Of course, when we play a college concert we can't be sure what's in the students' minds; perhaps they just like the music and aren't thinking about the religious aspect."

The Ward Singers' most cherished memory is that of their little-publicized trip last year to Vietnam. "The morale among the men was so great. The GI audiences seemed to be about 25% Negro. Everybody had a way of trying to keep us from feeling panicky. If we heard any disturbing noises they'd say, 'Don't worry, that's just range practice.' It wasn't until we got ready to leave that they finally told us, after we'd been sitting around waiting for several hours: the airport had been bombed and nothing could go out that day. We went back to our hotel. One U.S.-occupied building right down the street had been bombed. They had thrown a bomb into our hotel too, but it didn't go off, thank God. The next day we were glad to leave, but we were every bit as glad to have spent those three weeks there."

Vietnam, Japan, Okinawa and Korea were additional conquests in the long list of challenges met by the Ward Singers. They have lifted hearts and salved souls from Caesar's Palace to the Tennessee Ernie Ford Show, from a New York folknik room (the Bitter End) to a smart

Honolulu supper club. They shared a stage with Jack Benny for six weeks at the Ziegfeld in New York; hit the Democratic campaign trail in '64; opened up the college circuit with their jubilant sound. They have sung for enraptured teenagers at a high school grad night in Anaheim and brought joy to GIs in the Far East. Since she had the whole world in her hands, what ambition could conceivably remain that Miss Ward has yet to realize? Pondering this question, she came up with an answer that might have seemed startling in the long-gone days when Negro parents, stigmatizing jazz as profane music, enjoined their children from playing it or even listening to it.

"I'd be the happiest soul in the world," said Miss Ward, "if I could make a record some day with Duke Ellington or Count Basie."
—OCTOBER 1967

(Clara Ward died in Los Angeles, January 16, 1973 without fulfilling that ambition.)

Anita O'Day

Anita O'Day, who once earned $2,500. a week in nightclubs and $10,000. for each album, has spent most of the past year in obscurity, living with friends in a small California town called Hesperia. Not long ago she moved to a room without a telephone at a $3-a-night motel in North Hollywood. She then had no work except one night a week at Donte's; she had had no record contract in close to ten years. The lady, however, sings no blues. She would prefer to see her situation analyzed in positive terms:

Anita O'Day, one-time Gene Krupa and Stan Kenton band vocalist, has been set for a week at Ye Little Club in Beverly Hills, to be followed by a stint at Concerts By the Sea, the smart new jazz room in Redondo Beach. Joyce Selznick, discoverer of talent for several major studios, is interested in Miss O'Day's life story as a screen property.

Anita recently finished a role as a singer in MGM's *The Outfit* for producer Carter DeHaven. Her performance at the 1970 Berlin Jazz

Festival was released in the United States on BASF Records. Best of all, after a life that has taken in all the seamier elements of both *Lady Sings the Blues* and *They Shoot Horses, Don't They?* she is in incredibly good physical and spiritual shape, looks closer to a woman in her thirties than in her fifties, is singing with the same note-breaking, horn-like style and hip, husky sound that illuminated her first hit record, *Let Me Off Uptown* with Krupa in 1941.

Anita was the classic, prototypical premature hippie. A familiar image during the early years was that of the girl in the zoot suit—as she puts it. "The knees were 29 and the cuffs 16." But in one of her more memorable films, *Jazz on a Summer's Day,* a documentary of the 1958 Newport festival, she looked alluringly feminine in a big black straw hat ("real ostrich feathers—the hat cost more than the dress") and a sleeveless linen dress. It is perhaps more relevant that she has often worn a suit of psychological armor that is hard to penetrate. Yet under the brittle, sardonic surface and the fast hip talk you find a vulnerable, resilient, totally honest woman. She has chutzpah: when the FBI visited her prior to one of her dope busts, she put her hands over their guns and quietly said: "Gentlemen, please . . . they might go off."

I found her in the motel room, trim and cool, her hair still neatly styled to suit her small, oval face. While I glanced through a series of perfectly preserved scrapbooks dating back to her infancy, she provided verbal counterpoints.

Born Anita Colton, December 18, 1919, in Chicago ("I took the name O'Day because it was pig Latin for dough and I wanted to make some"), she boarded the career roller coaster early. "Ma and Pa were separated; she had to work, so I lived with her in one room and a kitchenette. I dropped out of high school and started entering walkathons."

The walkathon was scarcely less grueling than that coeval evil, the dance marathon. But the thirteen-year-old Anita, tall enough to enter the contests by lying about her age, literally took it in stride. "We had fifteen minutes' rest every hour, so it could have been worse. I finished second in four out of six contests. My longest walk took 3,428 hours. The prize was a percentage of the gate—a few hundred bucks to take home to mother."

At nineteen, after singing in local bars, she joined a combo at the Three Deuces and soon, digging the jazzmen around her, developed all her trademark qualities. Though her style did not emerge fully grown like Minerva from Jupiter's brow, the time spent absorbing the work of other singers was minimal; very soon she was her own self and a whole school of Anita O'Day-type vocalists developed. Later Kenton singers—June Christy, Chris Connor—were invariably compared with her.

She won *Esquire's* New Star Female Singer award in 1945, accepting her Esky statuette from Judy Garland in gala ceremonies at Los Angeles Philharmonic Auditorium. A couple of *Down Beat* poll victories came around the same time. Most of her hit records meant little to her, since the bandleaders paid her a flat fee: $7.50 each for *Let Me Off Uptown* and *That's What You Think* with Krupa (the latter was a unique, legato wordless blues), $50. from Kenton for *And Her Tears Flowed Like Wine*.

When the chance for a hit on her own came around, luck threw a curve. In 1953 she picked up an unknown song and recorded it for a small label. But *Vaya Con Dios* in the Anita O'Day version bombed out; it was Les Paul and Mary Ford who, after listening to her recording, cut their own version and turned it into a million-dollar smash. Grabbing the ring on the carousel may have been less important to Anita in those years than finding a connection. From the early days on the road with Krupa, she not only sang like a musician but talked and lived in a manner engendered by her social contacts. ''The narcotics thing was just there. It was what was happening. Kept me in and out of trouble for 20 years; cost me a couple of very nice houses, the Jaguar, the self-respect, everything. I got busted the first time for marijuana and served forty-five days. Next time was for pot again; I got ninety days but they gave me forty-five off for good behavior. These were misdemeanors, but the third time around, I got busted for heroin. That was a bum rap—a musician set me up for it; he was able to keep out of trouble by turning someone else in every so often. They put me in jail for six months. Well, I figured I had the name, I might as well play the game. So when I got out I decided to try it. That's how I got started. Boy, I really got involved. It's like quicksand—you never get out.

''They busted me for heroin again; that was in '53, and although there were no more busts, I didn't stay clean. Then one night in 1967 I went to some joint and took an OD and woke up at UCLA Medical Center, with five doctors standing over me, and one of them saying, 'Hey, girl, you've been out for six hours. You were almost gone.'

Somehow they brought me around, and I told myself, that's my cue.'' The time had come to get away from the environment. She took off for Honolulu and soaked up the sun.

The road back was blocked by a series of obstacles. During more than a decade with Verve Records she had been supported by the best arrangers and musicians Norman Granz's money could buy: Ralph Burns, Billy May, Bill Holman, Marty Paich, Gary McFarland, Cal Tjader. But her contract had run out, her name value had shrunk and there were no more offers. Major dental surgery cost her most of her teeth and money. Still another blow was the death in 1970 of her perennial agent, Joe Glaser. She was out on her own. "Except for John Poole, my drummer, and his wife—I was staying with them in Hesperia—I've had nobody really close to me since my mother died twenty years ago. There were two marriages; one to a drummer when I was very young, and one to a professional golfer that lasted twelve years. All through the panic days plenty of bread was coming in, but when you're young you don't think about saving money. Then when you're older you can't.''

Asked how she had managed to keep up her appearance and morale during the down years, she replied: ''You know, it gets to be so heavy, you just pack it all down and walk on top. In a way it's good that I don't get called so much for tours. For so long it was nothing but road, road, road—I've been traveling just about all my life, it seems. I finally told myself I had to sit somewhere quietly, and that's what I'm trying to do now.''

To those who know only the hard surface and the sophisticated manner it may come as a surprise that religion was a guide on her road back. ''I'm not a religious fanatic, but we all have our little beliefs.'' She reached across the table in the kitchen and read from a Presbyterian pamphlet called *Guideposts*. ''Listen to this. It says, 'No matter how unattractive or how dangerous the road ahead may be, it is better than the road backward. The road ahead may mean difficulties, but the road back means failure. You must teach yourself to regard the unknown as friendly, and remember that God is always at the end of the road ahead; but at the end of the road back you will only find yourself.'

''So,'' she said, ''you keep the spirit up and go right on. This is how I approach life. Not every minute, of course; but I worked last night, so I'm up today.''

—APRIL 1973

Jackie Cain & Roy Kral

Looking at them as they exchange tender glances, listening to them as they chant their way joyfully through a set at Shelly's Manne Hole or some other contemporary watering place, you may find it hard to believe: Jackie Cain and Roy Kral will celebrate their silver wedding anniversary next June; they have been singing together, in essentially the same airy, hip and high-spirited style, with undiminished taste and sensitivity, since Dave Garroway discovered them in a Chicago bar and sponsored them in several local concerts. At the time Paul McCartney was five; Harry Truman had served two years as President and the first postwar television sets had been on the market for just a few months.

The partnership that began in 1947, surviving several musical revolutions, has worked few changes in them. When Jackie shows you family photographs, you are reminded of those television commercials in which mother is mistaken for daughter. The early Sinatra cheekbones, the deep-set eyes, long blonde hair and perpetual look of mixed wonderment and discovery; nothing has changed in her except the dues paid. Nor would you detect the years that have gained on Roy Kral, except that he has traded in the crewcut for a mod look and the acoustic piano for an electric model.

"We've managed quite comfortably to get into a lot of new areas," said Kral. "When some of the first rock things came along they seemed too simplistic, but after the Beatles got into songs like *Yesterday* and *Norwegian Wood* we began ro appreciate them." Jackie added: "What turned us on to them was the records, and the enthusiasm, that our daughters brought home. At first we'd say, 'Well, uh, it's really not that great,' but hearing some of the songs over and over, we were converted."

The Krals were associated initially with the new jazz of the '40s. To their early fans they were a product of Charlie Ventura's "Bop for the People" combo, Roy playing boppish piano and joining in unison or harmony with Jackie's vocals on *Mountain Greenery*, *The Continental* or wordless versions of jazz instrumentals. Jackie's gentle solo vocals were perfectly tailored, as it turned out, for the East Side sophisticates: *Spring Can Really Hang You Up The Most* almost became her private property. Their good friend Alec Wilder supplied them with his songs and even wrote album notes for them.

After two stints with Ventura (1948-49 and 1953) they found their niche in the supper club circuit. A few years later they settled in Las Vegas. "The money was good," said Roy, "and we played all the right places—Lake Tahoe, Reno, San Francisco and back to the Sands or the Dunes or the Riviera; but Vegas became such a bore. Bad television, no movies; nothing but work and boredom." They picked up their lives and career, transplanted them to New York and in 1962 eased into a comfortable ten-year sublease in a 150-year-old house in Riverdale, overlooking the Hudson,. "The nightclub scene was fading," said Jackie, "and both our daughters were of school age, so we arranged to stay in town by getting into commercial jingle work."

Back in the 1950s, if you lived outside Manhattan and didn't happen to pick up on their occasional LPs, you might have reason to assume that the Krals had lapsed into oblivion; but theirs was a luxurious form of obscurity. "For one little bossa nova thing which we sang anonymously as a background to the pitch on a shampoo commercial," said Roy, "we made $50,000. Then there was a cereal spot for which I composed the song, wrote the arrangement and read the copy. They kept on running it, and it kept on supporting us, for at least two years. Residuals are wonderful. We'd spend summers on Fire Island, do occasional clubs and stay home with the kids."

The past two years have been the most traumatic of their lives. Roy was plagued by a persistent back ailment. Soon afterward, they went on their first European tour, badly mismatched with a group of hard-blowing jazzmen who attracted crowds completely out of sympathy with the Krals' subtle, often near-classical concepts. For the first time, after all the years of uninterrupted success, they met hostility and booing. (Kral: "We sounded too structured, too worldly-wise for those audiences; but after a few nights we changed our selections and things got better.") But that experience was a minor misfortune, a prelude to real tragedy.

Last May, five days after the family had moved into a new home in Montclair, New Jersey, their twenty-year-old daughter died in an automobile accident. A week later their drummer, long a close friend, was mysteriously killed.

Somehow the Krals have ridden out this critical time. The pain is not yet behind them, but they keep an eye on the future, work more clubs, write new songs. Jackie characterized one of their more recent works,

Heading, as "Our little fling at idealism." The upbeat message speaks of the open country, of leaving the city smells behind, of the search for peace, love and joy. It was written last year, before the loss of their daughter, but listening to them today, you know that the serenity and maturity reflected in their music is something that has helped to see them through.   —NOVEMBER 1973

Billy Eckstine

A few years ago Billy Eckstine recorded an album called *The Prime of My Life*. The title could have been used just as aptly this year, or thirty years ago; for Eckstine, every day of every year is prime time. Among the top-echelon singers who have the universal respect of their peers, Eckstine (known to friends simply as "B") has the longest and steadiest record. He had neither sunk into the pitfalls nor scaled the sort of peaks encountered by Sinatra. Things have leveled off comfortably. At a price of $7,500. to $10,000. a week, his agency has set 16 weeks for him in Nevada, regular visits to Europe or Australia, and occasional jobs near his Los Angeles home. It sounds luxurious and secure, as indeed, it is; but the assurance of work and money tells less than the whole story.

Like so many of his peers in the classic-pop idiom, he hasn't devised the formula for a hit record, though he knows how not to do it. "You take these kids," he says. "They're truthful with what they're doing. That's why it comes off good. But there's a record by Perry Como in which he uses a rock background, and it's absolutely ridiculous. It's just not Perry Como.

"Andy Williams, on television, geared himself to the younger set, which is admirable, but he too has done some things on record with backgrounds that just haven't come off, because they're not truthful. Same thing happened to me when I was with RCA; they had me doing *Condemned for Life With a Rock 'n' Roll Wife,* and *Tennessee Rock 'n'*

Roll, which I'm happy to say nobody bought, because they were the dumbest things I ever did. The A & R men hide behind that cliche about 'This is what the kids are buying.' It's an easy way out, but it doesn't work."

Billy Eckstine, in his fifties, is in impeccable physical shape—not an ounce of excess baggage—and his almond-shaped face suggests a man twenty years younger; the smile ready and warm, the speaking voice resonant and assured. Few who catch his shows nowadays are aware of his stature as a virtual founder of modern jazz. After leaving Earl Hines, he formed an orchestra, one that should have made a historical imprint. Sarah Vaughan was the other singer; Dizzy Gillespie, Miles Davis, Charlie Parker, Gene Ammons, Dexter Gordon, Art Blakey and a score of other giants passed through the ranks before he was forced to disband in 1947. It was the first big bebop band, musically apocalyptic but too far ahead of the public taste. Eckstine, still a hot property, went out on his own, no longer encumbered by a sixteen-man payroll, and many doors opened to him. Soon it was covertly admitted that his irresistable good looks and beguiling way with old Russ Columbo ballads—*You Call It Madness, Prisoner of Love*—had extended his audience to the white female upper classes. "They never let him become the sex symbol he could have been," says his longtime friend, composer Quincy Jones. "If he'd been white, the sky would have been the limit. As it was, he didn't even have his own radio or TV show, much less a movie career. He had to fight the system, so things never quite fell into place."

Still, by 1950 he was able to crack open one of the big rooms, the Desert Inn in Las Vegas. Nevada at that time was Mississippi with crap tables. "That was when they made all of us live across town in some dinky hotel. But you can check the files at the William Morris office and you'll see that as early as 1948 I had it written into my contract that I was to be treated as a guest at the hotel where I sang, and everybody was to be admitted. There were a few people who did this. Ellington was one. You did this as a man, out of a certain dignity you felt for yourself and for your race." As an early, quiet and unpublicized fighter for civil rights, he bridles at the attitude of certain Leroy-come-latelies, "the so-called spokesmen with the 'look-how-black-I-am' attitude. There were no TV cameras and reporters following us around when we went through those changes. Those supposedly knowledgeable blacks never made a Southern tour."

Only a few frustrations come to the surface. Once his agent, submitting him for a TV appearance, was turned down on the grounds that "Billy hasn't got anything in the charts." Eckstine reacted indignantly: "What the hell am I, a nine-day-wonder record act? I've been accepted as a household word as far as my contribution to music is concerned; I've been singing for a living since 1934 and making records for thirty years. Why should I still have to prove myself?"

High on his list of missions unaccomplished is the hosting of a nightly TV series. "I think I have all the qualifications. I've had enough education to be a good host; I'm well versed in world affairs, I know all about sports, I play several instruments. Other blacks have had a chance to do these shows, at least as substitute hosts; I've never even gotten that far. I've guested on all those programs. Some of the hosts have a background of only a few years in show business; if their guests aren't contemporary people they don't know what to talk to them about. So I go on and they say, 'B, how's your golf game?' Man. I'm sick of talking about golf!" (B has a 5 handicap.) Or they say, 'How many kids now?' This has been done so long that my kids are now old men!" (There are five boys, the eldest twenty-seven the youngest fourteen, and two girls twelve and ten. Bill Junior, twenty-two, is a Vietnam veteran.)

Eckstine admits to a special motive in seeking the television gig. "The chance to sit down here at home would enable me to go to school every day. I'm the only one in my family that doesn't have a degree. My mother and dad, in the old Negro family tradition, believed that education was the first step. So I had high school and a year of college. My sisters are both school-teachers in Pittsburgh; one of them has her doctorate. My parents have passed on, but until their dying day they respected the fact that I had made it on my own. Still, I could go further along the lines they had in mind for me. Right now I'm studying music, taking guitar lessons with George Van Eps."

With his attitude, William Clarence Eckstine can rest assured that the prime of his life has never quite been reached. Today, as always, it's just a couple of paces ahead.   —NOVEMBER 1970

(In March 1971 Eckstine began a series of monthly appearances as master of ceremonies for "The Jazz Show," which I produced for KNBC, Los Angeles. Despite excellent reviews, guest appearances by many prominent jazz combos and singers and an Emmy nomination, the program was never picked up by any other station and was dropped in 1972. His career since then, including occasional television guest appearances, has followed the pattern he described in 1970.)

Lena Horne

There are three faces, three facets of Lena Horne.

In recent years, Horne the entertainer has been busier than at any time since her voluntary semiretirement in the late 1960s. Beginning in May 1974, when they kicked off with a TV special in London, Tony Bennett and Lena worked together much of the time.

Back home in New York, the second Lena will take over: mother and grandmother, in an apartment just around the corner from Gail and Sidney Lumet ("I'm not a clinging mother-in-law, but I do live a great deal through them") and their two daughters, Amy, 8, and Jennie, 10.

The third Horne, never far below the surface, is a woman constantly in search of her identity, seeking knowledge, finding fulfillment through friendships and books and a devotion to social causes. She works with Delta Sigma Theta, a black women's social service sorority, and with the National Council of Negro Women.

She remains trim and exquisite. Every five years she seems to develop into a different kind of beauty, and if you have known her since she sang with Charlie Barnet's band in 1940, you cannot help marveling at this continual evolution. Chic in brown slacks, tan jacket and brown turtleneck sweater, stylish blue-rimmed glasses now framing the radiant eyes, she sits sipping coffee, reminiscing about the traumatic changes that brought her back. Within the span of a year or so, death claimed the three men closest to her: her father, then her only son, 29, and then in 1971 Lennie Hayton, who through a 23-year marriage had been her rock, her solace, a gently flowing fountain of knowledge and (to hear her tell it) her musical Svengali.

The triple blow was so intense that she says, "I still can't describe how I feel: I don't seem yet to have had the big reaction . . . I'm still afraid it might come. But I try not to think about it. I seem to have kept busy, busy, busy, since it happened."

Working with Bennett has been a breeze. "Tony and I get along so well—I guess it's because I admire and respect him. There's none of that show-biz friction or competitive feeling. That might be more likely if I worked opposite another woman singer.

"When we were booked for Boston and I heard about the busing situation, which was then at its height, I refused to go. Tony understood, of course, and went along with it, though it cost us I don't know how many thousands."

For all her strength, Lena has never had complete self-assurance as a singer, has always felt herself on the periphery of music. At last, she says, "I've made peace with myself and can now stand to hear some of the things I do. I've learned a lot in the craft, and I've quit wanting to commit suicide because of not being able to sound like Aretha Franklin, whom I adore, or Dionne Warwick.

"I read somewhere that Roberta Flack said I might not sound black to some people, but she thought I had a tremendous amount of soul. People never used to say that. I think it has grown in me and it's very gratifying."

Is she at heart a socially active person who continues to dabble in music, or vice versa? Lena laughed gently. "I think I'm continuing to dabble in music because it activates the use of the name for other purposes." The name has had some sort of box-office value ever since the early 1940s, when she stepped directly from Cafe Society in Greenwich Village to a Hollywood contract. There were several landmarks, most of which would be better forgotten. Aside from two early "all-colored" movies, *Stormy Weather* and *Cabin in the Sky,* her image during that decade was totally plastic—a sleek, aloof figure leaning against a pillar, taking singing parts in gaudy MGM musicals, parts that involved no acting and were chopped out when the films were shipped South.

The 1950s brought a different frustration: McCarthyism for

Lena meant seven years on the blacklist, unable to work in TV or films. "Sure," she says, "it hurt me financially; but it educated me to a lot of things. I began to grow as a person under the blacklist/redlist. I didn't torture myself about it, because it's never unusual for black people to have a bad time. Unlike Jean Muir, John Garfield and others whom it absolutely destroyed, I had a built-in alarm button. So I could find some dimension of that situation just in being what I had been from birth, you dig? I think the impact was blunted for me anyway; I was busy raising the kids, sending them to school, working in supper clubs, spending a year or so on Broadway in *Jamaica*."

Las Vegas was a frequent refuge from the '50s on, one to which she still repairs occasionally. "But the producers are strange. They say, 'My God, Lena, you're great, but why do you work so hard and have nothing going for you?' I ask them what they mean and they talk about 'producing' me, which entails vocal groups, sets, changes of clothes—the point being that people are so TV-oriented, so used to looking at that little box, where everything moves.

"That's the great thing about working these theaters with Tony; it doesn't bother our audiences to sit still and concentrate."

Working for dinner-digesters and drinker-gamblers has never been her style. Offstage and on, she is most at home among people who are deeply committed to music. Often she makes a point of her devotion to musicians, who she feels understand her better than others outside their special world. "While I was in New York with Tony, I recorded with Michel Legrand and all the guys—Richard Tee, Cornell Dupree, Ron Carter, Grady Tate—the giants! They are always very tender with me; they teach me. I did mostly Michel's songs, which are hell to sing, but wonderful. We also did a song by Bob Freedman, my conductor, who writes a great deal like Lennie."

So many avenues of conversation lead back to Lennie. From the start of that romance, in the mid-'40s, there were problems with which both of them had to come to terms; initially, opposition at the studio, where he was a musical director. "But we made another life . . . I miss traveling abroad nowadays, the way I used to, because I haven't found a way to look at something, admire it and have a Lennie to turn to and say, 'Look! Isn't it pretty! Isn't it good!' ''

For years Lena and Lennie lived in Hollywood. Later came a home in Palm Springs, a town that seemed peaceful to him, sedentary and lethargic to her. Today her place on Manhattan's Upper East Side precisely fits her needs. ''I never want to own a house again. I don't care to have possessions—which is just as well, because the week before Christmas I was robbed of all the jewelry my father left me. And I don't want to get married— God, no! I don't even think I was a particularly good wife. We loved each other and he certainly taught me everything, but I think if I had not been 'Lena,' I might have been a much better cook, better housekeeper.

''Lennie's very avoidance of any feeling that there was a difference between us sometimes irritated me. I'd say: 'But I am different! Some of me is, and some of that is admirable, and maybe that's what you like about me!' But basically I admired him for his attitude. It was an example of the kind of insulation musicians have. You just can't talk about them like you talk about real people. As much as I loved Lennie, I didn't care for a lot of his friends; and I asked myself, is it because they're white or is it just because I don't like these cats? I didn't know. But overall, I feel more comfortable and open with people than I did, just because I confronted myself with these questions.'' She insists that whatever strength she has shown was drawn from the men around her. ''My dad instilled in me, from the beginning, a willingness to accept the fact that some of the greatest things just couldn't happen for me. Everything inside me that was like him has protected me. Then Lennie certainly left me strong and knowledgeable enough to make a living, and my son Teddy, who was close to me in those last few years before he died, opened me up to being younger and wiser. I was very lucky to have three men who taught me so much.'' (Teddy Jones grew up mainly with his father, Lena's first husband; Gail stayed with her mother.)

She has learned to live beyond the bitternesses that could easily have engulfed her; for example, there was the irony that her first acting movie role, in a nonsegregated film, came at the age of 51 when she played opposite Richard Widmark in *Death of a Gun-*

fighter. She made no effort to follow up that belated fulfillment. "It was fun, and a challenge, because I hadn't practiced the craft of acting very much. I think if I hadn't had my other life as a singer, I might have pushed ahead; but my feeling at this point was that it was too little, too late."

And so, for an amazing proportion of the youthful strangers she meets backstage, Lena Horne is the lady they saw in a guest shot, playing herself, on *Sanford and Son*. Or she is the fabled symbol to whom young blacks say: "My mother told me about you. I just had to meet you."

For this incomparable product of the negro middle class, who grew up as a Brooklyn bourgeoise, the greatest source of joy now is the respect she has gained among the young, particularly among blacks who had to struggle even harder than she—people from whom, during her escapist years, she felt alienated. "There's a group of girls out here—Dionne, Lola Falana, Mary Wilson, others—who call themselves Bravo. Three years ago, when I opened with Billy Eckstine at the Circle Star Theater in the Bay Area, they came up there and gave me the most beautiful ring, from the whole group. They said I had been sort of a mother figure who had made all of them possible.

"To me, that was a tangible assertion that I am Lena Horne, a person—something I can put my finger on; if I may coin a word, let's say I am part of a generativity of my own young people. They said, 'While you're still alive, we want you to know this.' They knew about all the dues we paid way back when. Well, that's kind of a marvelous thing to happen, coming from my peers—and young ones. Hell, the Urban League can give me all the citations in the world, but when I see Aretha and we put our arms around each other, I really feel I'm part of the whole thing . . . I never did before."   —MARCH 1975

COMBO LEADERS

The Brubecks

Dave Brubeck, the catalytic innovator whose quartet indulged in so many harmonic experiments in the early 1950s, the pianist whose crashing crescendos and jaggedly unorthodox rhythms were the subject of so much critical controversy, today has a broader and more heterodox image, and is established as a serious composer of major works. First came The Light in the Wilderness, characterized as an ''oratorio for today,'' recorded with the Cincinnati Symphony and the Miami University A Cappella Singers. The text was adapted from the Scriptures by Brubeck and his wife Iola.

More recently there was the cantata, *Truth Is Fallen*, dedicated ''to the slain students of Kent State University and Jackson State, and all other innocent victims caught in the cross fire between repression and rebellion.'' Commissioned in 1971 by the Midland (Michigan) Symphony, it was recorded in 1972 with the Cincinnati Symphony, soprano Charlene Peterson, and a rock group called New Heavenly Blue, with Chris Brubeck on trombone, keyboard, vocals, and collaborating with his mother in the selection and adaptation of the text.

The closeness of the Brubeck family is manifested in many ways: a high point of the first Newport Jazz Festival/West in Los Angeles will be the concert ''Two Generations of Brubeck.''

It might well be entitled ''My Three Sons.'' Pianist Darius Brubeck, 25, has led his own avant-garde ensemble since 1969. Danny Brubeck, 18, will play drums with the group, and 21-year-old Chris Brubeck, leaving his regular rock combo home, will guest star as trombonist with Darius. (Less musically inclined are the two other junior Brubecks: Michael, 23, is involved with poetry, and Kathy, 19, is studying art.) ''We got into this family concert idea last year,'' says the 52-year-old patriarch. ''The reaction and the intergroup feeling have been so exciting that we plan to expand it. Of course, I carry my own regular rhythm section—Jack Six on bass and Alan Dawson on drums—and Gerry Mulligan will be with us. Carmen McRae will sing a couple of numbers with us—*Take Five,* also a song from *The Real Ambassadors,* which she did with us at the Monterey Festival in 1962.''

How the Brubeck family works in terms of idiomatic cross-fertilization varies greatly from concert to concert. ''If Darius is getting a particularly strong reaction to an avant-garde performance, his combo will stay on longer; otherwise, he may go into something that will bring Gerry Mulligan onstage, and the mood will change to a more conventional jazz thing. We just leave it open and mix in with one another whenever and however it feels right.'' Though the senior Brubeck clearly is the major box office attraction he has been delighted to find that at several concerts his sons have drawn even stronger applause than his own group. ''We played a college concert in New Jersey the other night and Darius' group broke it wide open. That was one night they didn't need any help from us old folks.'' The career of Darius Brubeck has taken off impressively; he has an album on Paramount Records, has done some film scoring and boasts a remarkable roster of sidemen. There is a certain symbolism in the contrast between the well-remembered alto sax sound of Paul Desmond in Dave's '50s-'60s quartet (light, floating, essentially melodic) and the far-out abstractions contributed to Darius' combo by clarinetist Perry Robinson, who is carrying the banner for a generation that has tended to leave this instrument in limbo. Dave's enthusiasm extends to another instrument in his son's group that never was a component of his own: the electric bass. ''He has a virtuoso bass player named David Dutemple who is just fantastic. I didn't realize until I heard him that anyone could progress so far. In fact, he's been booked to play a two-week gig in New York entirely on his own—jusrt solo bass, nothing else in the club.''

The cultural interchange has proven beneficial to both generations. One day at a rehearsal with the junior Brubecks, Dave found himself edging into a strong Latin rhythm. ''What I was doing demanded an emphatic four-beat drive from the bass and a real south-of-the-border groove. Well, you realize that this is something new to musicians who have come up in the rock era. Growing up in California, of course, I heard these things all the time, being around Mexican music. So once in a while I'll be surprised to find there's an element they're unfamiliar with, and they'll say 'Gee, that was great! On the other hand, they turn me on to things that I normally wouldn't use.''

"Would that be mostly in the electronic area?" I asked.

"This may surprise you, but the area in which my kids leave me way behind is far-out time signatures. It's strange, because we were associated with 'Take Five' and various meters that seemed very advanced ten years ago; but the youngsters can play with perfect ease in 7/4, 11/4, improvising even in 35/4, and they don't have to count any more than a jazz musician twenty years ago would need to count 4/4 time. Darius and Chris actually are finding extensions of areas I now realize I wanted to go into. But they may do this by referring back to something out of my own past. They'll say 'Look, Dad, when you want to play this, just think of *Unsquare Dance.*' That's a piece I wrote in 1961. It's a stimulating give-and-take. It works well with the audience, because many people will bring their kids, or sometimes the kids will bring their parents, and each of them can say, in effect, 'This is what I listen to, and I accept what you like.' So everyone benefits."

In August, the Darius Brubeck Quintet will embark on an expedition of its own, playing Israeli concert halls and kibbutzim. Shortly afterwards, Dave has a South American tour scheduled for which, he says, "They want just me and the three sons. In fact, more and more people are asking for us in that context, as a quartet.

"We tried it out recently under unusual circumstances. Kathy graduated from a school in Great Barrington. She's headed next for Sarah Lawrence. Well, they asked me to be the speaker, so Kathy, very embarrassed, asked me if I wanted to. I said I didn't think so. So she said, 'Well, I'd rather have you play. Would you do that?' And she wanted the three sons up there with me. All I said at the graduation was: 'This is going to be a very different speech.' I walked over to the piano and the four of us played the graduation speech over and over. Grandmothers who had taken all their children and grandchildren to graduations for twenty, thirty years were saying, 'This is the way to do it.'"

Stepping at once forward and backward, the Brubecks shortly will join forces for an album that will lend an avant-garde and/or rock touch to *Blue Rondo a La Turk, Three To Get Ready* and other modern classics from the *Time Out* album and era. The empathy among Brubecks senior and junior clearly transcends family considerations. Dave has been a mentor to his sons but never strictly a teacher. As Darius recently remarked, "He won't tell us 'Do this' or 'Don't do that.' But if we ask him a specific question, he'll always have a helpful answer. And he knows so much about programming, format, things like that.''

Dave Brubeck's only great regret is that the messages of his more ambitious works did not take root. "All I did with Louis Armstrong and the cast of *The Real Ambassadors* was point out the universality of music and cultural exchange. We did it as an LP and played excerpts at Monterey. But when I took it to David Merrick and a half a dozen others of his stature, they told me I was preaching. The show was never produced. The ironic part is a few years later, preaching and protesting were all around us; everyone was into messages on a much harder, more aggressive level.''

Brubeck should not feel frustrated. What he had to say—socially, politically, spiritually—in *The Real Ambassadors* and the other extended works in oratorio and cantata form reached hundreds of thousands via records, airplay and concerts. Besides, as the incident at his daughter's school made clear, his ambassadorial ventures, even without words, have had an impact on two generations and may be extended by still other gifted Brubecks yet to be born.   —JUNE 1973

Dizzy Gillespie

Dizzy Gillespie, who was the United States government's first official jazz emissary (his big band toured the Middle East for the State Department in 1956), represented America again in December of 1973 in Africa. Gillespie's quartet helped to celebrate the tenth anniversary of Kenya's independence, spent three days there and then gave two concerts in Tanzania. It was Dizzy's first visit to black Africa.

"I wrote a suite to be performed in a concert at the Kenyatta Conference Center," Gillespie said. "I'd agreed to take the gig provided they would find me a couple of the best local drummers. So I got over there, man, and they hadn't found me no drummers. I said, 'This is Africa and there aren't any drummers? Wait till I tell the cats back home about this!' Then I ran into an African conga player I'd met at Ronnie Scott's Club in London. He agreed to come to the rehearsal, and he brought a friend. They both played on my own conga drums.

"The reason behind this goes back to a conversation I had with President Nixon in 1969 when I was a guest at Duke Ellington's birthday party at the White House. The President told me, 'You did a fine job on your State Department tours; isn't it about time for you to go back and play again for your fans overseas?' I told him, 'Mr. President, I ain't too particular about playing *for* those people; I'm more interested in playing *with* them.' He said, 'Well, do they have that caliber of musician over there?' I said, 'You don't realize the worldwide extent and breadth of our music. I'm liable to walk into a club in Afghanistan and hear a guy playing a solo he took off one of my records note for note. Sometimes you can find a better musician for a certain job in a place like Osaka than you can get in Philadelphia.'"

In Nairobi, on Uhuru (Freedom) Day, Gillespie played his suite, dedicated to Prime Minister Kenyatta. He describes it as an incorporation of Indian, South American and African influences, with a touch of the blues for good measure. The work was entitled *Burning Spear*—Kenyatta's nickname many years ago.

The celebrations also included an unexpectedly agile performance by "Big Daddy" Idi Amin, the 270-pound president of Uganda who joined with the Masai tribal dancers and Kenyatta for some high-life high kicks. On being introduced to Kenyatta, Gillespie presented him with a record, a photograph and a plaque he had received for the occasion from a fellow member of the Baha'i faith, to which Dizzy has belonged for some years. "I met Haile Selassie and President Amin. I also shook the hand of the Aga Khan, who is doing some great things there, building hospitals and schools. Later, when my tooth started acting up in Dar Es Salaam, I went to his hospital.

"Some of our music may have sounded strange to the Africans, because harmonically they are still in the same place as always. Their music didn't sound unfamiliar to us, though; in fact, it sounded a lot like calypso. But when I said this to an African musician, his answer was, 'Wait a minute, man. It's the West Indians who sound like *us*—don't forget it all originated here.'"

It has often been observed by blacks from the United States visiting Africa that they become conscious there of their status as Americans just as fully as they become aware of their heritage as Afro-Americans. Gillespie and his sidemen (including guitarist Al Gafa, who is white) took delight in finding physical resemblances to friends in the United

States. "Every face all over the world is supposed to be unique, but wherever we turned, we'd see someone that reminded us of a cat back home. One day Mickey Roker, my drummer, said: 'Look, there goes a double for J.J. Johnson!' And I'd say, 'Hey, there's Cannonball Adderley!' Boy, that was a nice feeling.

Dizzy was given no State Department briefings, no instructions to be diplomatic. "If I was asked anything about the situation in America, the way I see it would be the way I'd say it. I was given no axes to grind." As a self-appointed duty in his diplomatic role, though English is the official language there he decided to address his Nairobi audience in their alternate African tongue with the help of a translator. This was the speech he delivered in his best Swahili:

"I want to say to all of you—the people of Kenya—that you have been my inspiration since way before independence . . . and also to say that this is the culmination, not only of my professional activities, but also of my human relationships . . . to come to Kenya, to perform for you, because I think of you as my people."

As Gillespie often says after some polysyllabic pronouncement at a nightclub back home: "Not bad for a South Ca'lina high school drop-out!"   —JANUARY 1974

Yusef Lateef

Yusef Lateef was born October 9, 1920 in Tennessee. In his fifties the composer-instrumentalist earned his bachelor's degree, majoring in flute, and now has his M.S. He will plunge forward with a Ph.D. in mind, switching to the study of philosophy at the New School for Social Research.

A tall, shaven-headed, quiet-voiced man, Lateef has the physique of a wrestler and the demeanor of a scholar. Reared in Detroit, he toured with name bands in the late '40s, achieving some prominence with Dizzy Gillespie's big band. Through the years he has had a thirst for knowledge, which many envy but few have the courage or find the time to emulate. In Detroit, he returned to his studies at Wayne University in 1955, and the program that led to his degrees began in 1965 at the Manhattan School of Music. Somehow he has managed to combine his academic interests with the life of a working musician, and has led various small combos for twenty years, except for a period (1962-4) when he toured with Cannonball Adderley.

"I've been fortunate," he says. "I went to school fulltime for five years and maintained the same group for most of that period, playing weekends or even full weeks in the New York area, and flying to various parts of the country for college concerts on weekends." Asked how his concentration on the academic life had affected his career, he said: "It's given me more insight, more feeling for the underlying principles of music. For example, while in school I composed a symphonic blues suite. It was recorded last month by the radio station orchestra of Cologne, Germany, and the U.S. premiere will be presented with the Detroit Symphony."

"Working regularly as you do with a small jazz group, don't you have the feeling, after completing such an ambitious project, that you're somewhat limited by what you have to do in clubs?"

Lateef bridled. "No. 1, I don't refer to my group as a jazz group. No. 2, the suite was written to feature the quartet; in Detroit we will have the combo plus the symphony orchestra, concerto grosso style, which will simply enhance the quartet." Pressed for an explanation of his objection to the word "jazz" (to which everyone from Duke Ellington down has taken exception at one time or another), he called it "ambiguous," adding that since what he is doing is anything but equivocal or obscure, an ambiguous term is inadequate. "If you must define my music, the true term is auto-physio-psychic music. That means music that comes from the physical, mental, spiritual and intellectual self. I did some research on the word 'jazz' for the dean of the Manhattan School of Music. Some of the definitions were downright insulting. I consulted Grove's dictionary of musical terms, Webster's and three others. One definition was vulgar. It said jazz means to copulate."

"I think," I said, "you'll find later editions have more accurate, sophisticated definitions."

"Which editions? Show me." I should have changed the subject. As lately as 1966, we found, the huge Webster's Third New International listed jazz not just as a noun, but first as a verb, followed by a windy musical definition mentioning syncopation and blue notes.

"What does that mean?" asked Yusef Lateef. "A note with a blue color? I take it literally. Notes are musical sounds. There's no color there. I've never seen the sound of music. It's something you listen to. As for syncopation, a lot of Prokofiev's music is syncopated, but it's not referred to as jazz. Yes, it's all vague, and it's done a lot of harm, dividing musicians and audiences, the same way mankind has said white man—black man and thereby divided mankind, instead of looking at men as just men.

"Let's say a group of people planned to go to a concert of music by Beethoven; if a sign were put up that it was jazz being played by John Doe, they'd be frightened away. I can't blame them, because if they looked in the dictionary and saw all those vulgar definitions, who would want to go and hear something like that? Some people only take things literally."

"I know," I said. "They wonder why blue notes aren't blue."

The point we both neglected to make is that dictionaries are lifeless documents; music defines itself. In any event, I suspect that avoiding the strictly musical connotation of the word "jazz" would be about as unnecessarily restrictive as never saying "paint" in discussing Picasso's techniques.

Mark Twain observed once that the right word is always a powerful agent: "Whenever we come upon one of those intensely right words in a book or newspaper, the resulting effect is physical as well as spiritual, and electrically prompt."

Rightly or wrongly, I have responded affirmatively for a long time, with electrical promptness, to the noun "jazz." Though I agree with Lateef about derelictions in dictionaries, I can hardly imagine myself working up a spiritual reaction on hearing the words "auto-physio-psychic music."   —AUGUST 1970

John Lewis/I

In a world wracked by violent change, obsessed with planned obsolescence, what price can be set on constancy? How valuable is loyalty
to an artistic credo? The questions might well be asked with regard to
the respected, world renowned Modern Jazz Quartet, masterminded
by the composer and pianist John Lewis.

The combo's newest member, Connie Kay, took over the drum
chair in 1955. With a different drummer, the other three—Lewis,
vibraharpist Milt Jackson and bassist Percy Heath—had begun working together in the winter of 1951-52. While a dozen rock and jazz
trends (and 1,000 small combos) have come and gone, Lewis & Co.
have remained almost untouched by the world around them, still
making the same delicate, pointillistic music. Over the years, however, John Lewis has lived a sort of double life. His extensive credentials gave him a key role in a series of ambitious large ensemble
ventures referred to as Third Stream Music. Some of these experiments
were conducted with a congress of classical and jazz musicians known
as Orchestra U.S.A., which played a season of concerts in New York
in the mid-1960s with Lewis as musical director. Others involved symphony orchestras and various groups in Europe and the United States,
collaborating with Lewis for concerts and recordings. The news that he
was to be honored by his alma mater, the University of New Mexico,
where his latest extended work would be premiered by the Albu-
querque Civic Symphony, with the composer conducting, came only
as confirmation of justice earned.

When he was in Hollywood to score two segments of Rod Serling's
Night Gallery, Lewis, a scholar and inordinately self-effacing man,
found it difficult to explain his ambivalence about his two worlds. "I
enjoyed the work, and I have nothing but the highest praise for the Los
Angeles musicians who perform in the studios. They're fantastic. I
find great satisfaction in writing, but I still enjoy playing and wouldn't
want to stop." I asked: "Would you consider eventually concentrating
on writing for television or motion pictures, or is that something you'd
just like to do once in a while?" Lewis hesitated: "I must admit I really
got hooked on television work this time around. But I can't even
consider breaking up the quartet."

"What can you say with the quartet that hasn't been said already?

Don't you sometimes feel the desire to expand it—find some new sound?" Lewis replied: "It won't work, it's too late—twenty years too late. People expect certain things of me. Even when I've changed the nature of the music a little, we've gotten in trouble, particularly in Europe—and our biggest market is in Europe, not here. When I went on a long European tour in 1964 with Laurindo Almeida, the Brazilian guitarist added to the group, there were some places where the audience didn't like the idea of our altering the basic sound. The quartet has been part of my career for twenty years now. You can't suddenly tear down your home where you've spent most of your adult life. Even if we didn't play any place except privately for our own pleasure, I'd have to do that. It's like an addiction."

Pleasing though it is, the MJQ no longer offers him a genuine challenge. He has several superior film scores to his credit, from the Belafonte *Odds Against Tomorrow* to Roger Vadim's *No Sun In Venice*. A couple of years ago he supplied the background for a 90-minute comedy by Paul Zindel for NET. He even had a fling at Broadway, writing incidental music for the William Inge play *Natural Affection*.

Lewis's sort of dilemma has faced many musicians. Torn between playing and composing, most of them have chosen composing, often as much for the greater financial as well as musical reawrds. Surely, for a man of Lewis's erudition and scope, a chance to work with the almost limitless resources of a studio orchestra must be like giving a painter a cathedral ceiling after two decades limited to cameos.

—NOVEMBER 1971

John Lewis/II

"The quartet has been part of my life for twenty years now. You can't suddenly tear down your home where you've spent most of your adult life . . ."

In retrospect there was a strangely prescient air to the interview. Headlined "Has Lewis Outgrown His Quartet?" it suggested that for a man of his great scope, broader horizons might be desirable. Now the unthinkable has happened: Lewis's playhouse is about to be torn down, his addiction kicked involuntarily. A few weeks ago, vibraphonist Milt Jackson, without whom the Modern Jazz Quartet would lose its identity, informed his colleagues of two decades that he was quitting. The group will play its last date July 17 in Australia. A four-way musical marriage that survived serenely through the most turbulent period in American history is now over because one partner insists on divorce.

Expressing his feelings in an angry outburst on a Los Angeles newscast, Jackson declared he has little to show for all those years, denounced what he called the overnight rock 'n' roll millionaires and implied that he was going out there to make some big bread. Good vibes? I didn't hear any. Jackson will be leaving three unhappy teammates, all of whom doubt that he has made a wise decision. None has any firm plans for the future, though Heath may form a group with his two brothers, Jimmy, a saxophonist, and Al (Tootie), a drummer. Connie Kay shrugged: "I could do studio work in New York, but I sure don't want to." Lewis, crushed, says: "The timing could not have been worse. I felt this most deeply when Duke Ellington died. To me his music was a significant part of my history and of growing up in America. His passing brought the importance of our quartet more clearly into focus."

Jackson's allegations, he says, have no validity in fact: "I think we made quite a remarkable living over the twenty-two years. As for the rock stars who earn the kind of money Milt is talking about, they are people in show business, entertainers. We are musicians. The com-Percy Heath said that in Germany the MJQ's concerts are presented as tax-free cultural events. "The U.S. government should subsidize artists of our caliber. At our age, we should have more to show for everything we've contributed." (Heath and Jackson are fifty one, Kay is forty five, Lewis fifty four.)

Monte Kay, Lewis's manager, says the quartet had a good year ahead: numerous bookings with symphony orchestras and various other dates, extending into 1975; an album, teaming the quartet with a symphonic ensemble, entitled *In Memoriam* (the irony was accidental), is due in the fall.

"The possibilities were so great," says Lewis, a quiet and gentle man whose voice, after a friendship of some thirty years, I have never heard lifted in anger. "There were four important extended compositions ready to work on. Now we'll never get to do them." That Lewis now is agonizing over a decision not of his making is doubly regrettable in view of the opportunities he turned down, sometimes for the sole reason that he would do nothing to jeopardize the combo's existence. He rejected an offer to write the score for *Sounder*. Years earlier he refused a chance to compose the music for *The Pawnbroker* (as a result of which the job went to a newcomer to Hollywood who thus earned his first major movie credit—Quincy Jones). "One reason I wouldn't do that, despite my respect for Sidney Lumet, was that I was too depressed by the story, which was about Harlem, where I lived when I first came to New York. It was like a nightmare up there, and after a year or two I moved away. *The Pawnbroker* just brought back those memories."

Now that fate has given him so many options, Lewis can go back to any of the several areas he has touched from time to time. His earlier film scores include important documentaries, one of them *Exposure,* the United Nations film dealing with the problems of refugees. Lewis has had numerous commercial and educational TV credits, the Broadway musical experience and original music for a ballet.

"I don't know what I'll do. My wife and I have talked things over. I had an offer to teach at City College in New York; Benny Goodman asked me to write a piece for him and a large orchestra; and I promised to write a piece for the Juilliard String Quartet."

When the dust has settled, this enormously talented man may conclude that the breakup of the MJQ was a blessing in disguise. The history of the quartet is, literally and uniquely, a matter of record. With one distinguished career behind him, and born late enough to look at Duke Ellington as a father figure, John Aaron Lewis can still find new challenges to meet, exciting pictures to paint, on a canvas far larger than the MJQ, for all its luminous beauty, was ever really able to afford him.   —JUNE 1974

(During 1975 John Lewis gave classes both at C.C.N.Y. and at Harvard, and recorded for Columbia with a specially assembled group.)

Shelly Manne

Shelly Manne, the drummer who is respected for his jazz accomplishments even more than he is envied for his commercial success as a
studio musician, arrived back in Hollywood recently from a visit to
Europe as leader of his avant-garde quintet.

Wearing a healthy Manne-tan and exuding good spirits, he turned in
an encouraging report. "It was seven years since I had really been
away from home," he said. "The tour rejuvenated me. It proved that a
jazz musician must get out on the road once in awhile. That's hard to do
when you're home and content and getting fat. Everybody needs a little
ego stimulus. You have to know, at first hand, that people do care
about what you're doing, and are listening and trying to understand.

"I'm 50 years old and I felt, 'What the hell, I'm going to have a ball.
I've got a young band and I'm proud of it, and at my age maybe it's the
last time I'll go out like this.' So we left enough time—we didn't just
rush from hotel to concert hall to airport day after day. The band had a
chance to breathe; they all played great and I think I played as well as I
ever have on a concert tour. The whole attitude was right, the lack of
pressure, and that feeling of being appreciated."

The discovery that somebody out there liked him was most happily
demonstrated during a visit to Italy. "The people there are so much
more aware of what our music really stands for. Most of the American
fans just don't have that deep aesthetic understanding of what jazz is all
about. In Italy they reaffirmed my faith in everything I'm doing. I met
fans who seem to own every record I've ever made; they know exactly
who played on each session and when it was made and what kind of
sticks I used. When you talk jazz with them, that's all they want to
hear. If you get into another area like rock, they don't want to know
about it. Rock has its own audiences, of course. I met many young
musicians who would rather get into jazz than rock, but often they're
frustrated because there aren't enough places for them to play. They go
right ahead and do their thing anyhow, often at a great financial
sacrifice."

Among his listeners Manne found college-age youths who related
immediately to the contemporary coloration his group has taken on
during the past year. Older fans, some in their sixties, attended the concerts, perhaps expecting to hear songs from his *My Fair Lady* hit album

of the 1950s, but remained open-minded and responsive when Manne tested them with abstract, original compositions.

"At one concert, in Verona, there were quite a few of these older fans," said Manne. "Teddy Wilson was on the bill with us, and every time he'd go into a tune like *Stompin' at the Savoy* or *Honeysuckle Rose* they'd burst into applause. It was a little rougher with my group doing unfamiliar material, but they still listened and seemed very aware. I think many of them felt that no matter how much identification a band may have with a certain style, it becomes necessary to keep expanding. You don't need to change forcibly, just evolve naturally.

"After the concert, the display of warmth was just beautiful. You walk into a restaurant and people stand up and applaud. Wow! It's so great to feel respected as an artist."

From the Italian Riviera the quintet flew to London for an eleven-day sitdown demonstration at Ronnie Scott's, the city's only modern jazz club. "They're making a real effort for jazz in England. They were doing a series of TV remotes out of Scott's club. I saw one of the programs, featuring the Kenny Clarke-Francy Boland big band. Kenny's the American drummer who has been living in France since 1956; Boland is a great Belgian composer and pianist. Their band is completely international. Well, I tell you, everything about that show was marvelous—the music, the sound, the color, the pacing—and no commercial interruptions. And this wasn't for an educational channel, it was on BBC! Can you imagine one of our networks giving over a whole program to a jazz orchestra?"

As it has for more than forty years, the printed word continues to work more diligently for jazz in Europe than in the States. "Look at this!" said Manne, holding up a major Italian newspaper. At the top of Page 2 of the main news section was an illustrated story heralding a visit by Manne's men and Duke Ellington's orchestra. "There are also several magazines that deal with jazz exclusively, and even a weekly pop music paper like the *Melody Maker*, which has a readership of more than a million, devotes several pages to jazz of every kind."

"What do you think can be done," I asked, "to create a situation that will be as inspiring to us over here as your experiences were over there?"

Manne played a two-bar finger-break on the coffee table before answering slowly: "I just don't know. The enthusiasm has to come from the fans. The performer can't concern himself with bending to play something he thinks people will like, because by doing that he's subconsciously killing his own creative powers. He has to play what he feels, and just hope it will be liked. Miles Davis did that and his latest LP sold close to a quarter of a million.

"I'll tell you another hopeful sign. There was this man in New York who has a son eleven years old. The kid played drums. When the father asked him where he'd like to go for his vacation, he said he wanted to come to Hollywood and meet me and see my club. It was the kind of situation you find in Europe, where the parents, if they're devoted jazz fans, pass their interest along to the children. This father was an old-time jazz buff with a big record collection, so the kid was well versed in everything from Charlie Parker and Dizzy Gillespie to Coleman Hawkins and Lester Young. I guess the solution, when you come right down to it, is for more kids to produce parents like that."

—AUGUST 1970

Gerry Mulligan

The image-makers, who operate as effectively and confusingly in the music world as in other areas of contemporary life, have been giving Gerry Mulligan more trouble than he feels he deserves.

Mulligan's has been an esteemed name in the evolution of modern jazz; first in Gene Krupa's band, then as key figure in the catalytic Miles Davis *Birth of the Cool* records, and throughout the 1950s as leader of a pianoless quartet (originally with Chet Baker on trumpet). In later years he divided his time between heading a thirteen-piece band and forming various small groups. Last July he put together a splendid group of musicians to play the opening day of the Newport/ New York Jazz Festival.

Despite all these accomplishments, the renowned baritone saxophonist says his role as leader is being ignored by the media. "I guess it's because I've been playing with Dave so much," he acknowledges. Off and on since 1968, when they toured Mexico and the United

States, Mulligan has appeared all over the world in an "extra added attraction" capacity with Dave Brubeck. "It's easy work. Dave just calls me up and says we've got to work on such and such a date. I don't have to spend days on the phone to find sidemen, the way I used to. But I've noticed, in recent years, my name was not even placed on the nomination list in the *Playboy* poll, in the voting for bandleader, or combo leader, or composer. For a couple of years my vanity was kind of piqued. I felt left out, hurt, but that was all. Then they did it again this year and I really got mad. Even if they didn't notice what I was doing in previous years, how could they not have known about Newport? Readers may look at these lists and assume I'm not active. By what set of rules are these nominations made up? This is the last thing I need just as I'm trying to become more involved on the school level."

Like so many jazz musicians lately, Mulligan is becoming concerned with the academics of jazz. "I've had a bunch of my scores assembled for publication, and I'm taking them out to schools wherever I can,. Man, I just love this kind of work. I spent a week at the Eastman School of Music in Rochester, did an improvisation class, got into a couple of arranging classes. The whole concept of teaching people to play jazz seemed such a far-out prospect, but in doing it myself I realized I could come up with a method that would really do these kids some good. I hear youngsters who can play a passable chorus on the blues—yet they can't play a song, can't get the meter straight on a melody! It's like arriving at a conclusion without making the journey."

Mulligan's album *Age of Steam*, released in 1972 on A. & M. Records, showed an extension of his early identity. He has not felt the need to change with the times by resorting to the fashionable innovations now popular with other saxophonists. "Our ears are being spoiled for the natural pleasures that used to exist. If you take the amplification away from a lot of what's going on now, you're left with nothing. In a civilization like ours, we haven't had time to absorb all the toys that have been handed to us, the inventions foisted on us. Despite all these electronic devices, I'm still intrigued by acoustical music, because that's where the fun and the challenge are. It's so much more interesting to get a bunch of good players together and see what sparks they can get off with one another, just with the natural sounds of the instruments."

As for the so-called "energy players," the saxophonists in whom brute force and stratosfreak tones seem to be the dominant elements, Mulligan says: "They fascinate me. Some of those guys do incredible things on their horns. However, my thing is primarily my involvement with my own music. In fact, I'm amazed sometimes at how little I listen to what is going on." This indication of his philosophy is consonant with a generally relaxed life and the pursuit of musical excellence. Though the days of point-provings are behind him, he continues to create, in a fashion that need never draw on any outside influences.

In the entire history of jazz only two men, Harry Carney and Mulligan, have attained a world-wide image as poll-winning baritone saxophonists. Gerry, who has been practicing lately on tenor, alto and soprano saxes and clarinet, says, "I wish I had the extra energy to carry all those horns around with me." But the virile, rugged baritone sound seems likely to remain his permanent, if not sole, identification.

Never an aggressive man, the Mulligan of today nevertheless conveys a revitalized sense of concern for his music. His decision to find new avenues as a pedagogue could not have been better timed; *Down Beat* recently estimated that no fewer than 390,000 Americans of school or college age are studying and playing jazz. After the years on the road, the idea of sitting down at a campus, expounding on one's music and performing it for open-eared audiences of pliable youths will seem more than ever desirable to many a touring musician; and it is for just such a role that Mulligan, one of the most articulate of men, seems ideally equipped.   —DECEMBER 1973

Charles Lloyd

"When I hear something that Charles Lloyd has written," said Bill Cosby, "it goes into the glands. The reason I dig him would be as deep as gland secretions. When I hear what I think is a humorous line played by Charles, I find it light and enjoyable. In some of the new wave jazz I hear obscurity and frustration and anger, but I don't want to go to a club and listen to an hour of it, uninterrupted. When you listen to, say, John Coltrane's *Meditation*—my goodness, you feel a hand is reaching into your body and gripping your bowels and just ripping them out. But with Charles, the whole answer is, he has a sense of humor."

What possible relevance can the reaction of a television comedian-actor have in an analysis of a musician and his work? Part of the answer is self-evident in the cogency of Cosby's remarks, part of it the conditions under which the comments were made. The scene was a dressing room at Desilu Studio during the shooting of a sequence for *I Spy*. The time was noon; Lloyd was due to show up momentarily for an appointment with Cosby's manager.

Patrons of the arts have come from every walk of life. Bach had the Duke of Weimar and Prince Leopold; Duke Ellington's salary in Prohibition days was multiplied by the syndicate boys who threw him $500. tips to play the *St. Louis Blues*. Leadbelly had his John Lomax, Benny Goodman his John Hammond. For the past couple of years Charles Lloyd has been subsidized, in recordings and other ventures, by George Avakian, the Brynner-bald former jazz critic and Thomas Edison of jazz A & R men. Now a second sponsor had set out to supplement, through his special power, what Avakian had achieved through financial and managerial guidance.

Well, who is Charles Lloyd? To such arbiters of American musical tastes as the aficionados of the Monkees—a cipher. But, to more explorative observers: a musical shock wave; a commanding mood manipulator who alternates between displays of savage visceral strength and interludes of gentle, loving warmth; a sartorial innovator; a communicative maverick in the alienated world of the jazz cosa nova. He is "the leader of a remarkable quartet . . . tall, slim, sparkling-eyed, with a smile full of a secret tenderness . . . a face-au-lait Trotsky . . . a remarkable flutist, a tenor saxophonist of extraordinary digital velocity and a bewitching tone . . . in spite of all the big prestige names, the seventh annual Antibes Jazz Festival would not have been worth the trip if it hadn't presented Lloyd.'' This report by Philippe Adler in *L'Express* was typical of dozens that have appeared on the Continent. Lloyd has earned the sempiternal prophet-without-honor cliches that have applied to jazz artists ever since Louis Armstrong first poked his head around the curtain on opening night at the London Palladium in 1932.

There have been modest successes at home. He has stolen a couple of jazz festivals. A few American writers have embraced him. Nevertheless, most of the thick wad of press reviews consists of ecstatic translations from Swedish and Norwegian, French and Finnish. (A deal earlier this year set him for a June appearance as the first jazz artist ever to be heard at the Bergen Festival.) At Antibes, the day after his wildly acclaimed festival debut, strangers passing him in the streets and on the beach, watching him walk into a restaurant would break into flutters of applause. Just forty-eight hours later, Lloyd was back for an opening at the Village Vanguard in New York. As he stepped to the bandstand for the first set, there were three customers in the room. ''In Europe Charles plays concerts; then he comes back here and has to sacrifice for night club gigs,'' said Bill Cosby, a former sit-in drummer from Philadelphia who has antennae more sensitive than those of many professional jazz experts.

Now, on a smog-free afternoon at Desilu, Charles Lloyd walked into the cramped dressing room. If he had nothing else going for him, his appearance would be a powerful factor. Down-turned mustache meeting a trim VanDyke beard; a circle of bouffant, natural-look hair; professorial metal-rimmed glasses; the inevitable waistcoat, and a style of clothing not quite Italian, not quite Edwardian, perhaps just Late Lloyd. (Feminine reactions to Lloyd, before he sounds the first A, have played a more than casual role in his impact.) Long-legged, gentle-mannered, he sat quietly, listening while Cosby reminisced. ''When I first saw Charles, he was with Chico Hamilton's Quintet. We enjoyed each other's company over dinner because we had so many of the same ideas. I've heard all his albums and watched him gain acceptance—some, but not enough. He hasn't changed as men change when they become leaders, except that his music is more powerful and personal than ever . . . Charles, I want you to meet my manager. Say hello to Roy Silver.''

As Lloyd, Cosby and Silver made small talk and played Lloyd LPs, discussed plans and took care of business, flashbacks ran through my mind, fragments of conversations with Lloyd, some with Avakian, with others close to him. Incongruously, blurred reminiscences came into focus in this spy-glass of a Hollywood studio, between takes during the taping of a sharp, cosmopolitan adventure story.

I was a screwed-up child. My father was a man who just couldn't cope with life. He was a pharmacist of sorts. I grew up very lonely. I was shipped off from Memphis to different places to live, to this old fat woman's house, to an aunt's, to my grandmother's place in Byhalia, Miss. My grandmother had bought that religion jive that society had laid on her; I had it too—you know, like they told all little black kids, be good to God and you'll have his blessings. They sold me the whole package. In Memphis, we lived in back of a drugstore, in a house on stilts. Under the house our dog would bark all night long, and sometimes dozens of other dogs would all converge, barking and howling while I just cried myself to sleep, nothing to look forward to . . .

AVAKIAN: "Charles's music is an astonishing combination of things that at first don't seem possible, yet it all works. It ranges from melodic and lyrical to wild and raucous; from orthodox modern jazz to abstractions, elements of Indian music, a wide range of Latin rhythms from calypso to bossa nova, a shouting kind of mainstream swinging, and sometimes, too, that underlying element of bedrock blues . . ."

Simple country blues was the first music I heard—that and church music. I was three years old, and I heard all those feelings coming out of all that oppression. I was nine years old when someone took me to hear Willie Mitchell's eighteen-piece band. They played those great arrangements out of the early Dizzy Gillespie book. It was such a shock; it knocked me out. Soon I was on the bop kick, having fantasies about Charlie Parker. I had an uncle in Chicago who was swinging pretty good in the paper department; he knew I wanted an alto sax and gave my mother the paper to buy it. I found you could get into the school band if you learned the school song. I spent two years learning all the songs of that type, as well as the St. Louis Blues March to play in a street parade. I blew all day and night and learned to play by ear. I was only twelve when I was called for my first gig, with Bobby "Blue" Bland's band. I was such a little fellow; I didn't have enough ass to fill out a coat hanger. Mother had to patch my suit together and fix me up with a white shirt and one Friday, after school, I went off to play this fish fry somewhere in Arkansas for four dollars.

It was a night I'll never forget. It took us five hours to cover the eighty miles in Bland's raggedy car. Bland kept asking me, "You know 'Peaches?' That's my theme, and if you mess it up I'll beat your ass." Well, I didn't know it, but after the gig he told me I'd played it better than anyone he'd ever heard—and I didn't even know which tune it was! The musicians seemed strange to me—hollering, eating fish sandwiches, drinking strawberry sodas, and all the time gambling. We got back in the car, and they stopped at West Memphis, Arkansas. Left me outside, in the car on this funky dirt road, while they gambled all day and all night in some joint. I was lying in that car crying, and quietly starving. Every once in a while I'd hear the sound of pistol shots in the air. When they finally came back, they were sore at me for being the only one that had money—they'd gambled all theirs away. Then they drove me back home. That was my maiden voyage in music.

For the next few years, until he was eighteen and left Memphis, Charles Lloyd survived—as most Southern Negroes do—by building a shell around himself. Within this isolation he found a degree of contentment through music. There were gigs, for $1.50 a night, with blues groups like Roosevelt Sykes and B.B. King's band. He studied with Irving Reason, leader of a local dance hall group. ("He had such love, the man sang through his horn like Bird.") He even got to work with Willie Mitchell, the hero he had discovered at the age of nine. There was no mixing; very few whites ever sat in with the black bands in the white dance halls where he played. All he knew about whites was the havoc they had brought into his mother's life and the opportunities they had wrested from his own . . .

After my parents broke up, my mother went with a very dark-complected man who owned a ghetto cafe. He had a juke box and live music. The cops came by all the time to pick up their graft; they intimidated this kind, good, gentle man who was keeping us alive. One night there was trouble in the cafe. A man stabbed a woman and killed her. Somehow the cops managed to tear the cafe owner apart—they tricked him into perjuring himself and then sent him off to the penitentiary. We'd go to see him in jail; his spirit was crushed, he was heartbroken.

Later on my mother met this Los Angeles-to-New York Pullman porter, and married him. I'd been an only child all that time; then when I was fourteen, after my mother married the porter, I had a half-

sister. My step-father was wonderful to me. He worked all kinds of jobs, sold cars and stuff, to make ends meet. He knew I wanted to study—I did all the reading I could in the library—and he knew I wanted all the music lessons I could take. Finally someone recommended a real good teacher, a man from Memphis who'd been to Juilliard. I was excited. I called him up and said I wanted to start right away. He listened and said, "Is this a nigger talking? I don't teach no niggers."

I began to study harmony on my own, and listened to more records. My mother was pregnant then with my half-sister. My mother had dreamed of sending me to college. The band director at high school had told me about USC. Because of my stepfather's railroad job I could get a free pass on the train, and somehow or other he got the tuition together. So one day I arrived in Los Angeles. I had a semester's tuition, fifteen dollars in cash, and a suitcase of cheap clothes. It was my first real contact with the world outside the ghetto. There was a traumatic experience when I auditioned on clarinet. I was the worst of the fourteen who auditioned, trying to play a Mozart concerto, competing against all those kids who'd had classical lessons. I thought to myself, this goes back to that emef who refused to teach me. I couldn't make those legit sounds. But I was determined not to be a goddamn drag. I was almost the only black kid out of thousands and we had nothing in common, but I had my fantasies to sustain me. Pretty soon I got to where I could play better than the guy I was studying with.

And that's how it went; mop the floors . . . clean up the football field; go to the restaurant: they need a bus boy. Claw your way through college—work in the evening, study at night, classes all day, sleep some time later. Saxophone and clarinet won't see you through; take up the flute. Study, listen, work, learn, create . . . I knew that the kids who'd gone on from Memphis to Tennessee State U. were having a ball, whereas at USC I had no social life. But I knew I was getting better training in European literature—Stravinsky, Bartok, Schoenberg—soaking it all in, and Eastern music too. I never felt sorry for myself; I was always too busy, always had a higher purpose in mind. I kept on the wheel. The years at USC changed my whole outlook on life. First I heard some guys talking Black Muslim style, and it really jarred me; stirred something up in me. But then I didn't really know any white people. Bitterness and hostility are spendthrift emotions. I soon realized nobody was my innate enemy.

After graduating in 1960 with a B average, Lloyd stayed on to work at his master's degree. By the time he earned it in 1961, he was rehearsing and jobbing around town with various bands. One day he had a call from Buddy Collette, the West Coast saxophonist.

COLLETTE: "I had worked with Chico Hamilton in 1956, and remained close to Chico. One night he called me; he needed a new saxophonist urgently. I had met Charles several times; he was lecturing now, and teaching music appreciation, at Dorsey High. But when I recommended him to Chico he gave it up and flew out the next day to join the quintet in Chicago. That was when Chico had the chamber jazz group, with the cello and guitar. Charles was playing alto sax, having fun and starting to develop; but after he switched to tenor sax, he really began to find himself. It was like he'd finally heard his own voice, and it was a voice of authority. Then, too, he found a real affinity with the guitar player, Gabor Szabo."

SZABO: "We talked about Charles's segregated background. He'd never had a white friend before, but of course right away he kiddingly said, "You're not white, you're Hungarian!" We found we were able to communicate immediately. Charles proves that when a person is content within himself, the antagonism disappears and he becomes a normal human being. He got his college degree, and within a year he was musical director for Chico, composer for the group, able to express himself. So his frustrations, though he still has them, have never been very deep-seated. Whether it's love or anger, a man's personality always comes out in his music. Charles incorporates elements that I've never heard any saxophonist achieve before. It can be a freedom sound, or a blues, an Indian kind of thing, or even something from the pop field; he puts his personal label on everything he touches, and he has the facility now to do on his horn absolutely anything he wants to. How many of us can say that? As for his humor, we know each other well enough to laugh about his eccentricities. He's not a phony and he wasn't putting the audience on at Monterey with that World War I Army tunic and the striped pants. It's all part of a game he plays. He doesn't take himself too seriously."

AVAKIAN: "When the representatives of the Bergen Festival were checking out the quartet, Charles and his men were very correct—ties, best black suits, white shirts; they could have been the Modern Jazz Quartet. Just as he believes in varying his musical moods, he likes to create all kinds of images of himself, and a variety of atmospheres—

literally as well as figuratively: at home, he likes to burn incense.''

* * * * * *

After reorienting the Hamilton group's style and leaving his permanent imprint on it, Lloyd left in 1964 to tour for a year and a half with Cannonball Adderley's sextet. Again his imprimatur was established on the personality of the combo. Adderley himself confessed that he was learning and bending in Lloyd's direction. But the job with Adderley was a pragmatic period of exposure before the mass jazz audience, a time of preparation for the total expression of his musical and personal concepts through his own group.

He has lived through three years as a leader, the first year a period of uncertainty, the second one of consolidation with a more stable personnel. Lloyd found an astonishing pianist, Keith Jarrett. Just twenty when he joined the quartet in February, 1966, Jarrett shared Lloyd's totality of vision and of technical command. He was already as far along pianistically as Art Tatum had been when Tatum died at forty-six; as far out, harmonically and emotionally, as Cecil Taylor, clambering from wild tone clusters to ferocious plucking at the piano strings; then moments later as down-home as Les McCann, playing the same brand of deep-dish blues Charles Lloyd had absorbed as a frightened, sensitive child in Memphis.

Jarrett is my kind of musician. No boundaries. We're trying to speak a universal language. I believe in complete fulfillment of expression, and our expression must be now. I am now. My drummer, Jack DeJohnette, and my bass player, Ron McClure . . . we all have this feeling. We're a group of believers, and our thoughts are cosmic. Like, music is the sacrament that can help us get through all the problems.

His philosophy of complete, constructive eclecticism explains the past success, present direction and limitless future of this colloquial mystic. Bobbing and weaving wildly as he plays, Lloyd communicates to his deeply committed audiences with wit and variety. He reaches out to find a chord for every crowd; this at a time in jazz history when the crypto-spiritual cliques, the walk-off-the bandstand syndrome, the mass hysteria of racial controversy, have trajected so many listeners from jazz into the arms of the folkniks and the rockers. Lloyd, almost alone among the avant-garde, is above the petty wars that have enveloped musicians and critics; where others have blown alienation through their horns, he has sounded a reassuring note of empathy. Though there have been times when he has had good cause to blame setbacks on race, his militancy remains constructive.

There's something I want to convey on a spiritual level; not preaching, and not just entertainment. I can feel the vibrations in the young people, especially in California. I played Fillmore Auditorium in San Francisco. The kids came there to hear a folk-rock group, the Butterfield Blues Band; but our message reached them. Maybe I'm the first to get to the psychedelic generation out of the jazz bag.

The Cosby-Silver conference had ended. "Well," said Silver, "looks like we're all set. This will be the first Bill Cosby TV Special, and we'll start taping around July. Original music composed and arranged by Charles Lloyd."

As he walked out of the studio gates, Lloyd's face was a mixture of elation and confusion. Was this in fact the turning point? Would the three customers at the cellar night club now expand into millions watching the tube? How would he fill the time and earn the paper during the months between? What would he say if his pianist were to ask him tomorrow how the quartet was fixed for next month?

I don't want the beer taverns; I don't need some guy in a beer joint to talk to me about where my thing is really at. I really need time, and my compositions must go on, man; something is speaking to us and we come to nature that way. Whatever our gift is, it musn't be negated by the beer taverns. I want freedom to sing my song. It should be presented where it's a total thing, a total experience. Man, it's a hard life if you don't weaken.

Since that afternoon on the *I Spy* set, Charles Lloyd has seen the first concrete signs of escape from the beer joints. The Quartet has played only four clubs since August 1966. The rest of the time has been taken up with college, ballroom and theater concerts, plus new triumphs in Europe. The key in the United States was the breakthrough at the Fillmore Auditorium in San Francisco, where Lloyd became the first jazz artist to play the "psychedelic light show" ballrooms and theaters.

On May 14, 1967 the Lloyd Quartet set another precedent, as the first American combo to participate in a Soviet Arts convention, at the Tallinn Jazz Festival and in Leningrad and Moscow.

The Tallinn experience was a cliff-hanger with a soap opera

finish. Newspaper readers in the United States and Western Europe were kept on edge day after day while Soviet officials who had invited Lloyd seemed to be having second thoughts about letting the public hear him. At one point the Quartet was canceled out at the very moment it was about to step up on the stage. On the final day, the group was permitted to play. The success was described by one Russian fan as "the end of the world." The explosion hit the front pages of several American newspapers.

The thunderous applause that swept the packed five-thousand-seat Tallinn Sports Palace lasted, according to one newsman's watch, eight minutes and twenty seconds. During that entire time, Festival officials were on the stage frantically calling for order through the public address system. "Tovarischi, tovarischi, let us behave ourselves.! . . . We are not children, we are adults . . ." Although Charles Lloyd had opened the program, a thirty-minute intermission was promptly announced and the house lights were turned up. Still the applause went on.

AVAKIAN: "At Tallinn the audience made you know that they had waited a lifetime to hear this music and they were grateful that we'd made it. It was overwhelming—an unrelenting physical pressure. American modern jazz has a bigger following in the Soviet Union than rock 'n' roll, and no American can appreciate the stiff dues the Soviet musicians and fans have paid to get where they have with their favorite music. There couldn't have been an audience anywhere in the world to whom our music meant as much as it did here. It made me realize how right we were to have made the trip, despite all the handicaps and road-blocks. We had to pay every cent of the cost from New York and back, except for the free meals and hotel rooms provided by the Festival. But we made history, and we gave those hungry people something they had never gotten before. We also realized that the Quartet's performance would have a tremendous beneficial effect for jazz in the Soviet Union.

"The last few months have taught me something I hadn't realized before—that the appeal of Charles Lloyd's music is limited only by people who *will not allow it to be heard*. Its universality transcends jazz. The same music which flipped the audience in Tallinn, Leningrad and Moscow has an equal effect on teenagers in California, and on the classically-oriented audiences who heard it in Bergen alongside Mozart, Bach, Beethoven and Verdi. Thanks to the open-mindedness of European government-sponsored television, millions of people have heard the Charles Lloyd Quartet in their homes in nine countries, including the Soviet Union, where no American jazz had ever been televised before. Yet when we came home from the most exciting, dramatic and historic trip that any American musicians have ever made to the Soviet Union—and I don't discount Van Cliburn's winning the Tchaikovsky Piano competition—we couldn't even get on a local educational TV show!''

COSBY: ''We have to make steps. We have to walk carefully en route to the rainbow. People like Charles must be presented. Here is an intelligent man who knows more about music than the average music teacher, has more talent than most top-rank musicians, and he has chosen this particular field because of bone marrow. So, he should be presented in concert, and on television, and wherever we can bring about something that will close the ignorance gap. That's the only thing. The only thing that's holding Charles Lloyd back—and others like him—is the ignorance gap. Let's hope we can live to see it closed.''   —OCTOBER 1967

(The promise shown at that stage of Charles Lloyd's career was not borne out by subsequent events. After devoting considerable time and money to his recordings and appearances, George Avakian turned to other interests. Lloyd all but disappeared from the music scene for a long while, then returned with a new group that placed a heavy accent on rock. Before his lapse into retirement Lloyd had flirted briefly with contemporary songwriting and recorded a vocal album.)

Terry Gibbs

The racial draft, an ill wind that blew thousands of black musicians out of jobs they deserved, has become a two-way undercurrent.

''At one time,'' said vibraphonist Terry Gibbs, ''when I was on the road with Woody Herman, the black musicians in the band had to stay in the bus or go to a ghetto hotel. All of us knew these conditions stank; we were powerless to correct them. Onstage, though, music was something we shared; our love for it was a common bond. Today everything is different—it's become a contest between black and white, a hatred thing, like 'What's this cat doing up there stealing my music?' If you want to talk about jazz as black music, as though it's something white people can only steal, then you'd have to classify all acting as 'white acting.' Sidney Poitier and Brock Peters had to look to someone for inspiration; perhaps Cagney or Jimmy Stewart or Gary Cooper—after all, who else were they going to emulate, Stepin Fetchit? But does that make Poitier or Peters a thief?''

Imbued with the desire for brotherhood, but confused by an apparent upsurge of hostility, Gibbs is in a situation typical of the social agony that has infiltrated jazz and popular music, areas once believed to be oases of inter-ethnic amity. He is especially concerned over complaints by a group of musicians regarding the lack of black jazz on television.

''That was special pleading. Their main interest was the avant-garde. They weren't representative of jazz in general. The fact is, TV should use a lot more middle-of-the-road modern jazz, black and white both. How often do you find Bill Evans, Herbie Mann, Stan Getz, Oscar Peterson, on network TV? In his heyday Dave Brubeck, who sold millions of records, had very little television exposure, so it's misleading for them to talk just about black music being kept off the air.'' Gibbs claimed that representatives of the campaign directed against the television industry do not speak for black jazzmen as a whole. ''One of them made a slurring remark about Buddy Rich. It's true Buddy gets more air time than most jazzmen, because he's a personality, but ask any black drummer, from Max Roach to Elvin Jones or Grady Tate; they'll all tell you that Buddy is also a phenomenal performer; and a lot of them have learned from him. Jazzmen have always dug one another and for years it was a happy, ungrudging give-and-take. My idols were men like Louis Armstrong, Duke, Benny Goodman, Dizzy, Charlie Parker—I guess about 90% of them were black. But what does black music mean? Lester Young and Benny Carter both said they learned a lot in their early days from a white saxophonist, Frankie Trumbauer; Barney Bigard still raves about Artie Shaw; Jimmy Hamilton was a Goodman disciple, and surely Bobby Hackett's horn made a powerful impact on both black and white musicians. Duke Ellington once said that Django Reinhardt was one of the three most original soloists in jazz history, along with Satchmo and Sidney Bechet.''

There is a sad irony in the present racial climate that puts men of goodwill on the defensive. Gibbs throughout his career has drawn freely on musicians of both races to work for him; this has meant, in effect, that his combos have usually been integrated. The sextet he leads on Steve Allen's syndicated TV show happens to be all white; Gibbs took over leadership after the group was formed, but admits he would be hard pressed to find better men regardless of race. ''For regular television jobs there ought to be a screening process. If a musician, black or white, says he can't get into the studios, a paired jury of top studio musicians should be formed—one white and one black trumpeter, and so forth; then let the applicants read the music, and the jury will pass on their overall qualifications. I'm sure that Clark Terry, if he were one of the judges, wouldn't say that a black player is good just because he's black, any more than a white cat on the jury would defend an incompetent white musician.''

Gibbs' suggestion should be put into action, as should any initiative that could compensate in some small way for the numberless injustices that have been visited on black musicians since the first years of live radio staff bands. Such moves will only partially eradicate the simmering discontent; nor can they restore the early spirit of mutual

''As recently as 1965,'' says Gibbs, ''right after the Watts riots, I had a call from Dizzy Gillespie. One of his musicians was ill. He asked me to fill in with him—at a nightclub right near Watts. It was supposed to be dangerous for white cats to go in that area. As far as I was concerned, it was one of the great honors of my career to be asked to play with Diz. I worked there for 10 days. All of us in the band got along beautifully, and the audience—almost all black—really grooved to the music.''

Gibbs regretfully concedes that today a black or even mixed nightclub crowd is about as easy for him to conjure up as a full-color image on a black-and-white film. He has seen discrimination from the other side of the fence. ''I've definitely lost out on jobs because I'm white. Nightclub operators have told my agent that I wouldn't draw any black people—which, sad to say, is true nowadays. There used to be black audiences for my music, and they seemed to be looser, more free with their reactions. I really miss that.'' More and more, polarization has become a fact of life in certain segments of the music world. Hard as this may be to live with, we must accept the grating truth that it will get worse before it gets better, if it ever does get better. The head-on collision between the cliche that music is color blind and the claim that some music is strictly black has created a problem that nobody, musicologist or sociologist, is about to work out until infinitely greater problems have been resolved that affect our multiracial society as a whole.   —JANUARY 1971

(In the fall of 1975 Gibbs said that he had noticed an improvement in the situation. "Because of the growing number of colleges, where black and white musicians are playing together in hundreds of big bands, the music is being judged more and more on its own merits. As for me, recently I played the Parisian Room, a Los Angeles club in a predominantly black neighborhood, and was received so well that I expect to be brought back soon and often. The black fellows in the club's resident group, who played for me, couldn't have been friendlier. Many well known black musicians came in the club to greet me.

"It's good to find things like this happening, and also to observe the great success enjoyed by a band like Thad Jones/Mel Lewis, with its completely interracial personnel. As I see it, the good feelings are really coming back.")

OTHER PLEASURES

David Amram

Renaissance, n: enthusiastic and vigorous activity along artistic and cultural lines, distinguished by a revival of interest in the past, by an increasing pursuit of learning, and by an imaginative response to broader horizons.

Not for nothing has David Amram been called a Renaissance man. His is the simultaneous pursuit of knowledge, of intercommunication among disparate areas of music and among their adherents. Above all, he takes infinite delight in being a part of all these phases and of persuading others to be as far ranging in their concerns as he is in his.

In his forties, his list of credits is staggering. He is the composer of an opera, *The Final Ingredient* seen on ABC-TV a few years ago; of innumerable scores for stage (the jazz-oriented music for Arthur Miller's *After the Fall*) and screen (*The Manchurian Candidate*, Elia Kazan's *The Arrangement*), of classical concert works; and has made countless forays into pop, rock and jazz. He has conducted and/or played with hundreds of symphony orchestras. In 1967 Leonard Bernstein chose him as the first composer-in-residence for the New York Philharmonic.

His is the kind of commitment that will move him, in the course of a single night, to conduct one of his own serious pieces with the Oakland Symphony, then to double as leader of a combo at a local coffee house, where he is apt to be found playing French horn, guitar or Pakistani flute. Amram is not out to make a multiple killing; he merely wants to see all musical worlds united, or at the very least sympathetic to one another.

The most compelling proof, not only of his versatility but of his success in deploying it, may be found in two RCA releases. In the first, a Red Seal album entitled *No More Walls* (the title tells the story), are his symphonic *Shakespearean Concerto*, the *Autobiography for Strings*, and lighter works reflecting Brazilian, Arabic and jazz influences. On the last two of the four sides Amram plays the guitar (which he took up at the suggestion of his friend and neighbor Bob Dylan), as well as the piano, kazoo, bouzouki and headbone.

The later LP, *Subway Night*, reveals him in the role of lyricist-songwriter-singer, with light overtones of rock. "It's almost a music education record," he says, "since the harmony is basically founded on simple guitar chords, and I used my symphony and jazz training in writing the orchestrations. Hopefully this offers a message to all kids playing guitars, that they're welcome in the worlds of jazz and classical music; it shows them that if they extend themselves and study more, they too can orchestrate their own things. Also, I hope it will encourage symphony players and conductors to get out and play and sing and really make music with the people."

In his spare time Amram conducts a group called Brooklyn Philharmonia, in youth concerts, using other musicians who are equally well versed in jazz and classical forms. "We sit in and play with the kids; they won't have this image of an uptight maestro—that old attitude where the conductor is a combination of the headwaiter at Ratner's and Adolf Hitler beating the musicians. We also play extended works for the kids such as Ellington's *Black, Brown & Beige*, right along with Beethoven, Mozart and Bartok, to impress on them that they all represent equally important contributions to the musical heritage of this or any other century."

Amram feels that certain classical critics have prevented this approach from spreading. "We did *Black, Brown & Beige*, at Philharmonic Hall in New York on the bill with Schubert, Haydn and a piece of mine. The audience and the kids in the orchestra loved it, but I doubt that a few classical critics there had any idea of what the music of Ellington is all about. They still can't accept the fact that it's possible for serious music to derive from a largely Afro-American cultural source. Even white jazz musicians are looked down on if they don't have a Ph.D. from Harvard or something, though they may be incredibly gifted writers like Gil Evans.

"Every jazz player I know is interested nowadays in modern classical compositions, in Arabic, Turkish, Indian and Oriental idioms—in any kind of music. But the converse doesn't apply. It's amazing how much they're missing that is fresh and beautiful and durable. If the classical critics can't hear what tremendously valuable works have been brought to us by men like Thelonious Monk and Charlie Parker and Bill Evans, they're denying themselves a great deal of pleasure. But perhaps it's not important, because the music is going to survive without their approval.

"A new generation of kids coming up now realizes that a great deal of indigenous American music has been shortchanged, overlooked and ignored by the musical establishment. All of it—jazz, folk, blues, gospel—should be presented and taught in every school. Some of the newer critics accept these facts. Their recent, belated interest in the music of Scott Joplin is a start; from there they just have to work their way up into what's happening now. They're only seven decades behind; give them time.''

Amram's crusade has kept him away from the movie studios. ''I never wanted to make a life's work out of that. When I was doing pictures like *The Young Savages* and *Splendor in the Grass,* using Harold Land and a lot of other jazz artists, it was hard even to get the studios to hire them. But at the time I lost interest in film scoring, men like Quincy Jones and Lalo Schifrin came along who shared that no-more-walls attitude; so now the whole scene is wide open.'' This, says Amram, is fine for those who are willing to be tied down to it; but as a free spirit he prefers to stay loose. ''I'm writing a violin concerto, working on more chamber pieces, conducting my music all over the country, doing what I can to bring together all these people from different worlds. Back when I was primarily involved in jazz, in the 1950s, there was a great spirit of everybody getting together and playing for the sheer pleasure of it. What we can do, those of us who were fortunate enough to come up in that era, is spread the same feeling among other people; not just in jazz but in every kind of music.''

Practicing or preaching, writing or performing, Amram is living up to these precepts. With the establishment of a few more such enthusiastic catalysts there will soon be no possibility for any music to function behind closed doors; the doors will no more need locks than atonality needs keys.   —APRIL 1973

Norman Granz

"Whenever there's any writing about jazz nowadays," said Norman Granz, in a voice clearly betraying irritation, "people dismiss me as though I were a retired man. Hell, right now, I'm promoting more jazz concerts than anyone else in the world, including George Wein."

One can understand his pique. Flashing back to the mid-1950s, you find yourself at a time when the American jazz world was Granz's blues-point oyster. Criss-crossing America with the "Jazz at the Philharmonic" concert package he had originated in 1944, recording dozens of live and studio dates for his own labels, he had brought the annual gross of Jazz at the Philharmonic Inc. up to around five million dollars. By 1957, several other concert units were trying to compete with him in the growing jazz marketplace; the American jazz festival phenomenon, conceived three years earlier at Newport, was gaining in size and prestige; but despite these developments the JATP tradition seemed indestructible.

Nevertheless, with a jarring abruptness, Granz that year gave up on the American concert scene. Two years later he took up residence in Switzerland. In 1960 he sold Verve Records to MGM for $2,750,000. Since then, the American auditoriums that were his stomping grounds have barely seen a trace of him. He is seldom in the United States for more than a few days, usually on business involving Ella Fitzgerald and/or Oscar Peterson, both of whom he still manages. Working from his home in Geneva or from apartments in London and Paris, he continued to tour JATP in Europe, but during the 1960s expanded more and more beyond the jam session concept, promoting appearances in England and on the continent by Duke Ellington, Ray Charles, Dave Brubeck and Count Basie. More recently he has financed such non-jazz attractions as Leonard Cohen, Richie Havens and the Mothers of Invention.

He returned to make one valedictory American whirl in 1967. With him were Benny Carter, the late Coleman Hawkins, and several of his old standbys such as Ella and Oscar. As the tour ended, he said: "Never again. I made a profit, but it's too much aggravation. It's no fun any more, at least not in the States." He has lived up to that promise, though he did appear at a nostalgic "Salute to JATP" evening staged last September at the Monterey Jazz Festival. His reasons for souring on the U.S. jazz scene: "The success of our concerts was due to the inter-mixing of musicians with contrasting ideas and styles, but the younger cats coming up don't like to jam informally. They all want to be leaders. That's all right for them, but it's contrary to the spirit of JATP. They talk about playing 'free jazz,' but what they play actually has a lot less freedom than the music of JATP."

Granz has kept in close touch, mostly via records, with the new post-JATP developments in jazz. In the early 1960s he brought John Coltrane and the late Eric Dolphy to Europe. He recalls meeting Ornette Coleman in Paris and discussing the possibility of sending him out on a Continental tour. "My reaction to his music is zero—whether it's some lack on my part or not, I really don't know. On the other hand, I don't care for what the Mothers of Invention are doing, either, but I feel strongly that certain artists at least deserve a hearing."

Today he maintains no office anywhere; as always, his main base of communication is the long distance telephone. On his occasional return trips to America he may be found in what was once the JATP headquarters in Beverly Hills, but is today the premises of Salle Productions (Ella's spelled backwards). During a recent visit, he summed up his attitude toward the current state of jazz. Although many American musicians who have toured Europe depict it as a jazz haven, Granz contests this view. "The scene is shrinking. Scandinavia is hopeless for jazz concerts now; they all want rock. Germany used to be an eight-to-ten-city tour; now it's four or five. In England and France there are no cities worth playing except London and Paris. Actually, America doesn't stack up too badly, in proportion to the population. But why should I promote jazz here? If I want to take the Los Angeles Music Center or Santa Monica Civic Auditorium, my rent is going to be the same as if I'd booked Creedence Clearwater, my ads will be just as expensive, so why gamble? You just can't come in and do a nice, quiet inexpensive jazz concert. In Hamburg the economics are such that you can play a hall seating only 1,700 and come out ahead with a jazz show. In a city of comparable size here, it would be impossible. There's more stability in Europe. You find the same successful people still enjoying the same reaction. Oscar, Miles, Erroll Garner will always do business. I've been bringing Ray Charles over every year for five years; Ella and Oscar annually for much longer; and Basie every year since I stopped bringing Duke."

During the mid-1960s Granz and Ellington were closely involved.

Perhaps inevitably, a relationship between two such strong individuals led to clashes and to a breakup in 1966. Granz says, elliptically, "Duke's story is that I discharged him. I was his unpaid manager for five or six years. Voluntarily I never took a penny in commission from him—I did it all as what I thought was my contribution to jazz. I heard the band recently, and for a lot of reasons I didn't care for it, but I still believe Duke's the greatest thing that ever happened to jazz." One of the more valuable products of the Granz-Ellington years was a TV special, shot during a festival at Juan-les-Pins. "I called it 'Duke Ellington at the Cote D'Azur with Ella Fitzgerald,'" says Granz. "One of the high points was a ten minute segment with Ellington, his bassist and drummer, and Joan Miro. They were shown surrounded by sculptures with Miro as guide, taking Duke around an art museum, the Fondation Maeght at St. Paul de Vence. I wrote a little script with Miro speaking in French, and Duke answering in English. It was aired twice in America on NET. When I have time, I want to edit it down to a forty-five-minute film. We had some tremendous footage on Johnny Hodges and Billy Strayhorn—probably the last before they died."

This venture, and the involvement with Miro, provided a clue to Grantz's broadened interest in the visual as well as the aural arts. "The best thing that's happened to me since I sold my record company," he said, "is that I have become a very close friend of Picasso. I ran my film for Pablo and he really dug it." Asked how many Picassos he owns, he replied, after a slight pause, "A lot . . . my entire collection of paintings is worth better than two million. Some are in London, some in Geneva, and many of them I have loaned out to museums."

In his fifties, though Granz may seem to lack the youthful aggressiveness that prompted his professional involvement with jazz, he is constantly active, working out the logistics of one Continental tour after another. If the artist is not to his particular taste, he simply finances the project and leaves the work to others; but when one of his preferred jazz attractions is due for a visit, he works with promoters in each city, who participate with him as partners or on a percentage basis.

"I'm touring Stan Kenton in January—Stan's first time under my auspices, in Europe," he said. "I just made a deal to bring over the Modern Jazz Quartet; also the Glenn Miller orchestra directed by Buddy DeFranco. So I'm as busy as it's possible to be. If I had the time or the inclination, I would get back into recording. Earlier this year I attempted to buy back Verve Records, but it didn't work out. Mo Ostin, a man I started in the record business, who today is president of Warner Brothers Records, tried to discourage me, saying, 'What for? Jazz doesn't sell.' But assuming all the conditions prevailing—today, I could run Verve profitably. This country has changed; the recording companies have changed. Executives nowadays are only concerned with the fact that they can gross $9 million with the Rolling Stones. They forget that a profit is still a profit, that you are still making money if you only net $9,000. I keep telling people that, and they think I'm crazy.

"Oscar Peterson, for example, is available. When I ask someone to record him, they want to know how much he sells and I'll tell them 25,000 or so, which would be profitable—but they don't want to hear about it. It's a disgrace what the jazz artists today are being forced to do, recording material that is all wrong for them. I let them try it with Ella a year or so ago and they wanted to create a new image for her by having her work the Fillmore, to promote the album of pop songs she'd recorded. I said, 'What for? She's making half a million a year as she is, why should I change that?' If I had my way Ella would never make another record—at least not by those standards. Who gives a damn? It's criminal, too, that someone like Sarah Vaughan was allowed to go without making a single record for five years. It's an outrage that of the twenty-seven albums I produced with Art Tatum for Verve, not a single one is available—they've all been deleted from the catalogue. The son of a bitch who did that ought to be hung from the nearest lamppost. I even tried to buy the Tatum masters back, just so I could get them on the market again, but they wouldn't let me have them. They'll never sell the rights to anything, and yet they won't make it available to the public. And you wonder why I don't want to come back?''

Granz's disenchantment is not simply with the state of jazz or the record business, but with American society as he sees it. "I could make more money in America, but life in a typical American city is far less fruitful and full than in London or Geneva. I'm unrooted; I'm a European. It's impossible for me to think of a single thing in America to bring me back that I can't find in Europe.''

Perhaps it is just as well that Norman Granz gave up on the U.S. jazz world when he did. He had an idea whose time had come, and he knew just how long to sustain it. Had he decided to continue JATP domestically into the 1960s, let alone the '70s, it is inconceivable that there could have been any consequence other than an anticlimactic winding down.

He quit while the quitting was good, leaving an ineradicable mark. Though his courage and initiatives are missed, American jazz to this day is the stronger for having experienced his presence.

—JANUARY 1972

(By 1974 Norman Granz not only had retrieved the Art Tatum masters, but had an active new label of his own, Pablo Records, on which they were reissued. During 1975 he was often in Los Angeles recording new mainstream-modern sessions for Pablo.)

Quincy Jones

Quincy Delight Jones Jr. celebrated his birthday a couple of months ago—mainly by showing his delight in being alive, specifically by starting off a tour that began that day in San Francisco and recently ended in Japan.

Showing no aftereffects of the two brain aneurysms that took him halfway through death's door, the former Hollywood studio wonder boy, who quit the movie music writing dodge after 40 major credits, is belatedly basking in the success that enveloped him last year, when "Body Heat" became his biggest album ever. Gold, of course.

Touring conditions are rigorous at best, but Q. (his music business nickname) was unfazed; he looks and feels healthier than ever. "I'm going to yoga classes six days a week, 90 minutes a day. I have a lot of respect for my body that I never had before. Not that I could have stopped what happened to me; the thing I had was with me from the day I was born, and there was no way a doctor could have foreseen that those blood vessels would pop."

Although "Body Heat" was primarily a collection of songs, with all manner of fashionable appurtenances (vocal group, great banks of electric keyboards and guitars and bass men, only a few horns), he was able to satisfy the Japanese audiences who knew him well from his days as leader of a big jazz orchestra. "Those people are so wide open, so open; they love a challenge. It's great to have a cat over in one corner calling for *Stockholm Sweetenin'*, which I wrote back in the '50s, and someone else shouting for *Everything Must Change*."

The touring band (three singers, 12 players) gives Q. added flexibility, he claims. Asked whether he didn't miss the openings for subtle voicings of flute and saxophones, and all the other trademarks of his big band years, he said: "Some of it I do miss; but that's something I've done already.

"With the big band I had an impossible situation on my hands. I kept saying, 'I'll never do it again!'—well, I tried, and I lied. I did do it again and again, but it's not only the economic problem that has finally ruled it out. It's seeing the cats grow—watching them run off and fly away on their own, the way Freddie Hubbard has since he worked with me, or Bob James, Hubert Laws, and all the rest who are stars in their own right now. I can't hire them any more, and once you've heard a sound like they can produce, it messes up your mind for anything less. So you just have to start building another house."

The new, streamlined residence is no one-room shack; Quincy points with pride to several unknowns who may be tomorrow's Hubbards and Laws. "We had an incredible Fender bass player, Louis Johnson. For his age, he has ears and a mind that are as fast as any bass player America has ever seen. He celebrated his 20th birthday during the Japanese tour.

"We had a young saxophonist named Ernie Krivda, who was recommended to me by Cannonball Adderley; and along with cats like this, we still have a couple of our old standbys like Frank Rosolino." (A big band graduate of the Krupa and early Kenton days, Rosolino is a next-to-incomparable jazz trombonist.)

Communication between the generations was no problem. "When I met Louis Johnson, it took us a while to discover how to talk to each other; but he's incredibly bright. At their age, it's important to give cats like that some input of our knowledge. If we don't show them a direction, they might eventually set up a culture entirely on the other side of the track and we'd be sitting on this side saying we're not into what you're doing, while they're saying they're not into what we're doing.

"I don't believe in that Hatfield-McCoy situation in any kind of music. If Louis Johnson wants to play one of those long, one-chord things, Ray Brown can show him how to stay five minutes on that chord and make it interesting; but he can handle something more than that. He'd listen to some of us playing Thelonious Monk's 'Round Midnight,' which has complicated chord changes, and he'd sit on the floor and listen and learn it in no time at all. He simply was never taught to assume anything is difficult, so he does it."

While dealing so efficiently with these representatives on the future, Q. is thoroughly wrapped up in a deep exploration of the past. His magnum opus, still in work, is an extended composition that will try to examine every aspect of African and Afro-American music.

"I'm so curious about everything. I've been digging back into history—not just back in the American thing, but all the way to Haiti and Trinidad and further back to the Berbers and the Moors.

"It's going to be long enough for an 80-minute, two-record album. We'll perform it live with a symphony orchestra, a gospel choir; a concerto grosso kind of thing with instrumental and vocal soloists.

"Working on this evolution story is like going back to school. A professor at the University of Massachusetts told me I ought to take all this information I'm gathering and write it up as a thesis to get a degree. Man, I don't know what I'd do with a degree."

Soaking up all the knowledge, living all the life he can after finding out the hard way how precious it is, Quincy continues his many-pronged attack on music, picking out tunes for another pop LP for A&M, preparing to go on a national tour starting in late June. He has even gone back to his first love, the trumpet, which he picked up on the last few nights in Japan. ("With these metal plates and two clips in my head, they'll have to demagnetize my horn.")

With all of his anxiety to keep working and determination to stay healthy, he simply will not permit himself to write another film score.

Says the man whose music and songs for *In Cold Blood, In the Heat of the Night, For Love of Ivy* and dozens more converted him from a respected composer-arranger into a hot Hollywood property: "I've had several very tempting offers, but I've turned them all down. I quite cold turkey!"

The movie and TV world's loss is the concert halls' and the recording studios' gain. It is good to have Quincy live and alive, in our midst again after too many years of seclusion, locked behind studio doors. —JUNE 1975

Marian McPartland

Not since Mary Lou Williams first came out of Kansas City has a musician struck as effective a blow for women's ad lib as Marian McPartland. She has had a series of successes as pianist, songwriter, educator and recently as owner of a company, Halcyon Records, that releases her own and other recordings.

In the summer of 1974 she took part in the Nice Jazz Festival, a predominantly traditionalist and mainstream event in which she was the only essentially modern musician; yet she managed to fit with ease into a variety of settings, playing with her good friend and ex-husband Jimmy McPartland, the cornetist; with the veteran violinist Joe Venuti; as a piano soloist; and in a two-piano set with Earl "Fatha" Hines, who had been one of her idols during her formative years in England.

The following conversation took place in Nice on the morning after her appearance with Hines.

FEATHER: It was quite remarkable to hear you with your lifelong hero, trading tunes with him, even playing his own composition—in fact, in the opinion of some listeners, you even outplayed him on his own tune.

McPARTLAND: You're kidding! Well, I had a feeling we were going to get into that song; I knew that someone in the crowd would holler out for *Rosetta,* so I wasn't too unready when it came time to do it. Actually, that's one of the things I grew up on, hearing Earl Hines play that.

L.F.: What interests me is that you are the only modern musician who has been here all week, yet you've managed to fit into all the different contexts. Even in your own solo set you played remarkable variety of works representing various eras, but with your own sound and style.

Did that just happen, or was it cultivated?

M.M.: I think it just developed naturally. I feel the early stages of my life in the States, when I worked in Chicago with Jimmy, really provided a good foundation. In the trade groups, playing with him, if I hadn't already learned some of the songs by osmosis from hearing them on the BBC, I learned them with Jimmy. I know all those old things like *Shim-Me-Sha-Wabble* and *Sister Kate*, and they're fun. The first place I played in New York was Eddie Condon's; I sat in there the night we arrived. It's all partly a state of mind, too, because I went through a period of being very narrow, when I was at the Hickory House on Fifty-Second Street, thinking that you must play what is au courant, and anything else is either old fashioned or you're not with it. I went through all that, but I got over it.

L.F.: But basically I'd assume you are more interested in playing things like *Freedom Jazz Dance*, right?

M.M.: Yes; what I like to do is play with a lot of harmonic freedom. I love to work with a free kind of group; not the sort of thing where everybody just makes noise, but where you're actually building something interesting, in an atonal context. It really can be done beautifully if everybody listens to everybody else. It's been fun playing here with some of the people I've never had a chance to play with before. Bill Coleman, that great trumpeter who's been living in France for so many years. George Barnes—we hadn't played together for ages. We used to play at parties, doing the same kinds of things we were doing here, little contrapuntal things, making musical jokes; that can really be very stimulating.

L.F.: You live in several worlds now. You're part of what might be called the East Side jazz world, but you also have your academic world with all the teaching you've been doing . . .

M.M.: The thing that's nice about it is, I don't think of what I do as teaching. It's incredible—I'm such an unschooled musician! [Not so. She studied theory and piano at the Guildhall School of Music in London, won a scholarship in composition, and at other times studied violin and singing.] A lot of things I do that I call teaching are really just a matter of exposing kids to music by trial and error, showing them how to perform or how to listen. As you work with different groups, you learn the sort of things you can do for them and what they can best relate to.

I guess I do have more than one world to deal with, especially when you think of this little record company; that's a whole other thing. But they all dovetail. For instance, when I'm working at an East Side club, I usually make an arrangement with somebody there to sell the records for me, and all jazz musicians who have their own label can do this; it's really a great short cut. Then the school thing—well, I just thought it would be nice to take the experiences I had in Washington, a nine-week project in black schools, and maybe try to put some of it down on an educational record with some of the teachers there. It was really incredible that I would be the one who was asked to do a project in the city schools, which are almost one hundred per cent black, and here I come, an English, white, female jazz musician.

L.F.: Didn't you once say you had three strikes against you?

M.M.: *You* said it! It was when I first came to America. Maybe you set up a kind of challenge whereby I thought, well, we can't allow these things to be detrimental; and they never were. Of course, I was never in the position of waiting to be hired, because I had my own trio, so I could call up the guys and hire *them*. So I guess I was women's libbing it long before there was a name for it, and I didn't think about it, or think it was anything strange. Gloria Steinem once said to me, ''Oh, what you must have gone through!'' I said, well, I really didn't; I don't remember going through anything terribly bad. It always seemed like an advantage to be a woman. I don't know if I suffered salary-wise. I always managed to get good guys to work for me. That's what is so great, to be able to look back and think of all the fellows I had in the trio at one time or another—Steve Swallow, Pete La Roca, Joe Morello, Bill Crow, Eddie Gomez.

So many great talents have come up over the years; and I still hear them. Doing the school thing I hear so many potentially terrific young kids, and I often wonder what's going to happen to them, and whether there will be enough teachers around to point them in the right direction.

In a way that's what my whole school thing was about; it was a pilot program in which I was supposed to involve all the local Washington musicians and galvanize them into some sort of interest in keeping an ongoing program in the Washington schools; it has been successful, and they are keeping the program going.

L.F.: Under what organization was that?

M.M.: The National Endowment for the Arts. They put up a huge hunk of money. It went through a high school principal, who handled the money, and then part of the money went for materials and teachers. I got part of it for my own salary and for paying local musicians; then we had money for instruments, rental of a good piano and so forth, and part of the rest went for guest artists—for instance, we had Billy Taylor bring his trio.

One thing I always wanted—and I decided that if this program ever materialized I was going to do it—was to arrange for Duke Ellington to come there and play; and we did. He had a date in Washington— this was in February, and he wasn't too well even then—he was going to play at George Washington University. I called his manager and said what about Duke staying over? Well, Duke happened to have a day off the next day, so he stayed.

The kids saw him. We had already prepared them with records, and taught them to do a little playing. They don't have musical instruments in elementary schools; all they have are these things called melody bells, a little instrument that you play like vibes, with mallets. Until we played them some records, these kids had never heard of Duke Ellington. A black music educator had told me that most black children don't know anything about jazz, that they just listen to rock stations. But after they'd seen him and heard him they became terribly involved. When he died they all took it very personally; all the kids who had been at that concert were extremely upset. They all wrote letters to Mercer and Ruth Ellington. I really felt as if we had accomplished something good there.

I enjoy working in all these different worlds. Pretty soon I'll be doing my East Side thing again, at Michael's Pub in New York; then I'll be in Florida for a couple of weeks because the Michael's Pub guy has just bought a hotel there. Also I'll be doing a week in a college here and there; a week in an elementary school in Long Island; and two days at a college in North Dakota.

L.F.: Are those combination recitals and clinics?

M.M.: Yes. It's got to the point now where I can play alone, and that means it's not such a big budget for them if they don't have to hire a trio. If they like, they can have me work with their college band. I've got band arrangements, things by Ernie Wilkins, Thad's compositions such as *A Child Is Born*, a couple by Dave Baker, and a lot of stuff of my own. I can either play these things with the school orchestra or play alone, and sometimes they want me to play, say, all Rodgers and Hart, because somebody's giving a course on that kind of music. There are so many different ways you can do these things.

In Washington, the culmination of the entire project came about through the cooperation of the Navy. We were able to get Constitution Hall, and the Navy bussed in 3500 kids to hear us play with the Navy band. We used fifty of the kids we'd worked with, had them come up onstage; we had an arrangement of *Things Ain't What They Used To Be*, and *A Child Is Born*, and *C Jam Blues*. And we had the kids join in and sing and play.

This really was the high point of the whole nine weeks, because they really had wanted us to demonstrate publicly that we were actually able to show kids how to play some jazz. We got two ten-year-olds who were outrageously uninhibited, and they came out front and improvised on *C Jam Blues*. It wasn't the greatest thing you ever heard, but for ten-year-olds it wasn't bad! You really live for moments like that.

—AUGUST 1974

Phil Moore

Sitting in the main room of a spacious office suite, one floor up in an old Hollywood duplex building, Phil Moore looks out at the Sunset Strip; facing the site of the house he once shared with Dorothy Dandridge, a couple of social revolutions ago. His fame as a vocal coach—the man who brought Marilyn Monroe and Ava Gardner and Diahann Carroll out of their shells—has tended to obscure his achievements as the carrier of the first flag for blacks in screenwriting on the West Coast, and radio network composing on the East.

Back in the 1930s, a confident kid from Seattle who was sure he had it made because he had worked in speakeasies for a steady $21. a week, Phil Moore came to Hollywood to conquer the city. It was a very different Hollywood then—especially if you were black. You were virtually banished to the ghetto. No restaurant or hotel would admit you. After one credit in a shoestring all-black movie (*The Duke Is Tops,* 1938, starring Lena Horne), Moore tried in vain to land a job as orchestrator at Metro, but was thrown a crumb; they let him work as a rehearsal pianist. "Even that," he recalls, "was a shock down at the old segregated black musicians' local. They couldn't believe MGM had hired a black guy. After I graduated to orchestration, they wouldn't even let me write for strings for almost a year; a black man wasn't supposed to be able to do that, even if he had studied at the University of Washington. But I became an instant authority on Africa, exotica, South America, jungles. That's why I have this huge research library today; I had to find those things out myself."

Frustrated by the limitations of his assignments—"I was Johnny Green's, Georgie Stoll's, everybody's assistant"—and the failure to receive any screen credits, Moore took off for New York. "If you can only go so far and then you bump your head—well, you just move over to something else." Something else turned out to be another series of firsts: talent director for CBS radio, chief arranger at NBC radio, pianist-vocalist with the Phil Moore Four combo that had a long run at Cafe Society. "I was also the first black to produce records for several white companies, on both coasts."

His image as a singers' trainer began through a long association with Lena Horne. "I like working with singers; it's a great challenge to mold personalities, come up with ideas. It's like being a gardener. You know the kind of seed, where to plant it. Music is the soil for singers to grow from. You see to it that they don't get too much sunlight, knock off some of the bugs, put up a little pole for support; but you can't make them grow. You just take care of them, cultivate them, and that's what I've done."

The list of artists for whom Moore composed, conducted, arranged, coached, wrote special material or shaped entire acts is astonishing: Sinatra, Garland, Bassey, Tom Jones, Pearl Bailey, Tallulah Bankhead, Roberta Peters, Bobby Short, Louis Armstrong, Perry Como. A few evoke special memories.

"Marilyn Monroe was sent to me by her manager to open up a new facet of her talent—singing. She'd been dropped by several studios. She told people I gave her enough confidence to do a music audition for Fox; then she got in *Gentlemen Prefer*

Blondes. She was very lonely at the time. In fact, she got me into trouble with Dorothy Dandridge. I'd be in my studio trying to shave and here was Marilyn hanging around when Dorothy comes up the back steps, asking, 'Well, do you do this with all your clients?'

"There were many parallels between those two. In certain people there are destructive qualities that get the best of them. Dorothy was very dear to me. Her life was like an apple that looked so beautiful, but when you bit into it, it was rotten. Here was a lovely girl in a wonderful home, getting integrated parts in movies at a time when even Lena Horne was only given roles that could be cut out in the South. But Dorothy's famous marriage—to one of the Nicholas brothers—had gone bad, and she had a retarded child. I helped switch the lack of self-assurance, the negative forces in her, into a positive thing. It's like changing an airplane motor, when you brake it by using that huge power to slow it down. However, when it's three in the morning and they're alone, the negative comes welling up again. It was the same way exactly with Marilyn."

Among the others whose paths crossed with Moore's:

Ava Gardner: "She had plenty of nerve on almost any level, but the microphone was as terrifying to her as a snake. Arthur Freed was convinced she couldn't sing, and she wanted to prove he was wrong. So I taught her to use her own voice for *Showboat* in a totally darkened room where she couldn't see the mike."

Roberta Peters: "A classical singer who wanted to do pop concerts. She 'oversang' in the typical operatic manner. I coached her in using less bravura, without losing her beautiful natural quality. Her pop concerts were a great success."

Mae West: "She liked to have a trumpet play the melody very close to her ear, to make sure she sang in tune. She had to have this assurance and I gave it to her."

Goldie Hawn: "The approach I brought to working with her was for that of an actress who was performing the lyrics of each song. If the Vegas reaction is any criterion, it worked. But they overproduced her show. When you put her onstage with a thirty-six-piece orchestra, and four boys and three girls dancing around her, it's like trying to see a flower in the Grand Canyon."

Diahann Carroll: "I remember when we had to sweat out a situation on the *Tonight Show*: She never got to do anything but sing, because they wouldn't have blacks on the panel. Finally she just had to stand up on her hind legs and say: 'Listen, unless I get on the talk part of the show, I'm not going on.' And they let her do it.''

Judy Garland: ''When I was in my rehearsal pianist days at MGM and had to work with Judy, they'd always send a chaperone along—I guess they thought I was about to rape her. But pretty soon they got over those fears.''

Today's Hollywood looks less inhibiting, more inviting to Phil Moore. ''I was very comfortable in the East. Had a nice business going in New York, a house in the country, composer-in-residence at the University of Connecticut. But I had a lot to say musically that couldn't be done in New York, because these days the music business is out here in Los Angeles. Quincy Jones kept bugging me: 'You can get credit now.' So I stayed here—after a 14-year absence.''

He and his son, Phil Moore III, who studied at Berklee College of Music, are learning from each other. ''He's into electronic music, so here I am messing with the arp synthesizer. This fusion will be helpful as we get into film scores, commercials, etc. And I've had more experience dealing with artists, so maybe he can get something from me. I'm proud to be working with a talented son. He's done a couple of pictures himself—with credit.''

Moore is not greatly taken with the wave of black films. ''It's good that black audiences can see black actors doing their thing. However, the first time you see a black guy haul off and hit a white, okay; but this can wear thin. Soon it's gonna settle down to where people will demand decent pictures instead of black exploitation. You can't be surprised at what's happened, though. How long have the cowboys been killing the Indians? When has our country not been violence-prone? American tastes change slowly.

''The opportunities out here now, in terms of the range of writing, are immeasurably improved. You can try anything. Producers and audiences alike want to hear new concepts.'' He is bristling with news of plans completed or projected. ''I just scored a 90-minute TV drama, *The Sty of the Blind Pig*. It has a lot of gospel music and luckily in New York I worked with the

Community Choir because I wanted to learn about that kind of scoring.

"I just finished recording an album—I don't know how the hell we're gonna sell it—on Gertrude Stein. I boiled down some of her writing, put a voice on it and music behind it. I'm working on another album now to celebrate the 2,000th anniversary of Catullus, the Roman poet. Catullus was the man who wrote an attack on Caesar. The guy who did the translation from the Latin has put it into street talk. It's very esoteric. Also, I've been preparing a one-woman show for Alexis Smith. A very bright lady, who wears clothes beautifully and sings well. She could be the next glamor object in the Dietrich tradition. We'll present her in person, but we may kick off with a TV show."

Much of the diversity of Phil Moore's life in music has been due to his prolonged absence from Hollywood. "Do you think," I asked, "if you'd been able to get credits as a screenwriter, you would have stayed with that career, without ever being side-tracked?" Moore paused. "In a way, I think being black has been very good for me. If I weren't black, probably I would have become a studio music director, with a big house and pool, and would never have worked at CBS, NBC—or at BBC, where I had my own radio program, coming on right after Winston Churchill's. Sure, if I'd been white I'd have had a really good position, and that would have been the end of it; but as it is, I've worked in every field except the circus. I had one great advantage over the average black kid. My mother never told me what I couldn't do. She'd say, 'Well, if you want to be President, there's only one at a time, so you gotta be pretty smart, but go ahead and try.' So my eyes were never on the ground. Also, it's a reward to know that you've opened up a territory, doing a good enough job so that after you leave they hire a second black. But it is frustrating. The reason hypertension is one of the great diseases among black men is that trying to operate in the white world you have to have your antennae out all the time. I had to know that when I saw an ad 'Come to Tahoe,' they didn't mean me, or 'Come to the So-and-So Golf Club' didn't mean me. But I see great progress. If you have the money, you can live pretty much anywhere you like. And plenty of black composers are working, though unless they're very careful they may be shoved into black films. The typecasting still exists. I'm a very blessed guy in that whenever I reach down within myself, something musical comes out.''

The story of Phil Moore, a man of extraordinary talent and versatility, would surely make a better biography or movie than many that have been successfully published. In a sense it is almost a distillation of the black experience in Hollywood over the past thirty-five years. One can only empathize with him for the reasons that caused him to leave, and rejoice at what seems to be his permanent return.

—MARCH 1974

Romano Mussolini

''One of the first piano players I heard was Fats Waller, because my father was an admirer of Fats Waller.''

Not a very unusual statement; the kind, in fact, that a reporter might elicit from a typical second-generation music lover. A little more noteworthy, though, when you know—could even guess from the speaker's jutting jawline and stocky figure—that the father referred to was Benito Mussolini. The remark was made backstage at the Pasadena Civic Auditorium, where his son was box-office bait for an Italian language vaudeville-and-jazz concert.

The traumas that have scarred the life of Romano Mussolini are hidden well below the surface. During several hours' conversation devoted almost exclusively to music, the only detectable hints were in a couple of elliptical answers: He began playing piano in 1942, but didn't start working at it regularly until 1956 ''because I was afraid to play in public.'' He told me music is not really a profession; he just plays for pleasure. ''In Italy is not easy to be strictly professional jazz musician. In my life, with the name of the family, is very difficult. So I have had many other jobs, always without a profit.'' A statement of fact rather than a bitter commentary; yet the youngest son of the Duce, who was all of 11 years old when World War II broke out, still has the self-deprecating air, if not of a loser, certainly of a man engaged in a constant search for identity, for security and impartial recognition of whatever talents are his.

If he were interviewed without revealing his name, his story would resemble that of any typical jazz-hooked youngster growing up in prewar Europe. ''I was lucky to be born in a country where all music is very popular. As in most Italian families, music was a tradition in ours. My father played the violin; never professionally, but he read music. My older sister started on piano, my brother Vittorio took up cello. It's odd—they studied but do not play; I didn't study, but I play.

''Vittorio was one of Italy's pioneer critics of jazz; he was writing articles about it in the early 1930s. One of the first records I ever heard him play was Duke Ellington's *Black Beauty*. So I started to love this music when I was three or four years old. I remember the first time I heard a Louis Armstrong record, the sound was so beautiful that I cried. The first influential pianist for me as well as the first big band sensation, was and still is Ellington. But I studied all the records—Teddy Wilson of the early Benny Goodman quartets, Fats and Earl Hines. When I was fifteen, I taught myself to copy them. It's very difficult to study piano without music.''

His father, instead of recoiling from the youngster's involvement with jazz, shared his interest. ''He and the whole family loved first the traditional folk music, the symphony, the opera and then, logically, the new music of the time, jazz,'' Romano recalls. The period referred to preceded and coincided with the war.

How do you talk today to a Mussolini who in the spring of 1945 was young enough to be innocently uninvolved, yet old enough to know of the events that reached their climax in Milan? If Romano Mussolini's memory has not blocked out those days, he elects to speak as if it had. World War II entered our conversation only as the time when he first heard records of the new jazz, the bop movement, and was able to amass a vast collection of V-Discs and 78s.

"I was also reading Panassie, Delaunay—everything about jazz in English, French and Italian that I could lay my hands on. When I met a U.S. Army officer for the first time, it was a big shock for me, because I spoke to him only about jazz—I said, 'Where is Duke Ellington now?'—and his reply was 'Who is Duke Ellington?' All he knew was Guy Lombardo. This I couldn't understand."

For a year after the war, the cadet and his mother and sister were confined to the island of Ischia. "The only center of jazz was a barbershop where we gathered and had sessions. I played guitar a little." Back in Rome, he was soon sidelined again, this time by pneumonia and a year-long convalescence. He completed his education at the University of Naples, studying economic science. "After I came out of the university, my first job was in a nightclub with a quartet. The pay was 300 lire, which was then worth $3."

There followed a long period of aimlessness. A postwar demand for wood led him to dealing in lumber. Later he got into the construction business with a friend, but "today my friend has millions of dollars, and I'm no longer in the business." After a series of other abortive ventures (among them a couple of years as a poultry farmer), his old friend Arrigo Polillo, a lawyer and jazz critic-entrepreneur, persuaded him to appear at a festival in San Remo. By then (1956) the Mussolini name evoked, for a new generation, more curiosity than emotional or political reactions.

"I didn't want to go, but Polillo told me it was good for jazz, good publicity for the festival; so, to help jazz, I appeared. Because of all the journalists and photographers, I was uncomfortable, but for the festival it was fantastic. Headlines in all the papers, 'Romano Mussolini Plays Jazz.' " Since that ice-breaking occasion he has been intermittently involved with music as performer, producer of jazz albums and promoter. "For three summers, 1960-62, I presented jazz at the Mediterranean beach resort of Viareggio. We had musicians from many European countries—America too; I spent one whole summer season playing with Chet Baker. "My first session playing on the radio was with Dizzy Gillespie. Dizzy is a kind man, so good-hearted; he became a true friend."

Though music has enabled him to travel extensively in Canada, Mexico and Australia, there have been sporadic side ventures. In 1969 he produced two films. "They were based on cartoon characters like Barbarella; full-length pictures, but not successful. I wrote the music for them also. Now when I go back to Italy I must write the music for two more films. One is a gangster story of the early 30s, with Dixieland and New Orleans jazz. I have been invited to direct a film—a movie about horse racing, very popular in Italy."

Visiting the United States with Mussolini for a brief tour (San Francisco, Pasadena and San Diego) was an old friend, Carlo Loffredo, an ex-lawyer turned bassist. Music in the Mussolini manner is eclectic, mainly in debt to Oscar Peterson and other influences of the 1950s. He is not about to win any jazz polls, but neither will he ever let any rhythm team down. More than any other impulse, the desire to belong, to be an unpretentious, swinging part of a jazz happening, suffused his solos in the old Charlie Parker blues *Now's The Time* and in *Sweet Georgia Brown*. The Pasadena audience received him warmly.

Spare moments during his journey were taken up by a visit to Shelly's Manne Hole to hear Bill Evans ("Fantastic!"), a quick hop to Las Vegas for an evening with the Count Basie Band ("Very disappointing—Frank Wess and Frank Foster and all the soloists of the 1950's have left him"), and a night at Donte's in North Hollywood, where the band of Louis Bellson (nee Luigi Balassoni) left him limp with excitement. ("We must arrange for him to tour Italy!") He is not partial to free jazz or protest music. "I like some things in it, but there's too much confusion. What is a musical protest? I think it is difficult to make a protest in music; it becomes easy to make anarchy, and then it's no longer music. My taste is for jazz that swings—the bass player walking like Ray Brown, the drummer not too loud as so many are today."

He speaks with pride of the keen musical ear of his wife, Maria Scicolone. "She sings with my group sometimes, but not professionally. We'll never forget the night she sang with Oscar Peterson. Oscar and I are—*come si dice?*—good buddies." Maria's·sister, Sophia Loren, is no less informed musically than the rest of the family. According to her brother-in-law, "Sophia

could be one of the best European jazz singers if she wanted to;
but she has other things to think of."

Having survived one visit here unscathed, he would like to
return under more desirable circumstances. Because of the Italian
variety-show setting, he was heard by few of the listeners he
most wanted to impress. "I'd like to play here in a jazz club,
where the audience and atmosphere would be so much better; but
there are many difficulties to obtain permission to work."

Difficulties, you conclude, have shaped a major part of the adult
years of Romano Mussolini, through one of the most devastating
accidents of birth that could have befallen an infant born in this century.

—MARCH 1970

Oliver Nelson I

Toting a saxophone and a septet across hottest Africa is a task
seldom sought out by American jazzmen, and just as rarely assigned.
During eight weeks of trekking through eight West and Central African
countries under the aegis of the United States State Department, Oliver
Nelson learned as much as he taught. The teaching was subliminal; his
combo played concerts at which most of the music was highly sophisticated by African and even Afro-American standards. The
learning was mainly a realization of social and psychological gaps.

"A lot of us were thinking of Africa as a way to go back to our roots,
to a homeland," said Nelson, "but we felt strange. They would say
'Parlez-vous francais?' and when we told them our French wasn't that
good, they'd say. 'Oh! Americans!' We met Negroes in the Peace
Corps who had gone to Africa to find themselves, but they couldn't
identify the way they'd expected to. They found a culture so different
and so unchanging that they realized it was impossible to become a part
of the African community."

The French-speaking countries on the itinerary, all of them independent since 1960, were the Central African Republic, Cameroon,
Chad, Niger, Upper Volta, Mali and Senegal. An exception was
Gambia, the former British colony which tweaked the lion's tail for
the final and decisive time in 1965.

The band played for three distinct kinds of groups. "We did concerts for the All-African elite, usually Catholic, often missionaries who got into government—the ones who have control of media such as radio and newspapers. They limited their enthusiasm to compliments after the show. 'Oh, it was formidable, fantastic!' they'd say, but with reserve. It was very different when we'd play for students. Every time we got through, we were just about mobbed. They'd rush on the bandstand, knock over saxophones and plead for autographs and our addresses. Writing out addresses became so tiring we finally had 10,000 cards printed at our own expense."

In a third category were free concerts for the man off the street, the type not advanced enough to understand anything but high life or traditional music. "These people are supposed to be completely un-educated, but they may speak a dozen African dialects. They responded, just like the students—applause, not just at the end of the tune, but during high points of the solos." For these audiences, Nelson changed the program a little. Aware that the flute is pervasively important in Africa, he let saxophonist Ernie Watts loose on an extended flute solo. "Ernie got in every lick that he felt would reach them, and he never missed."

Reactions differed little from country to country. "There was one upset in Buea, a British-language town in normally French-speaking Cameroon, and do you know how the people in Buea acted? Just like the English people! We were seventy-five percent of the way through the concert before they responded to anything. After the show an announcement was made that the concert was over, and the audience meekly formed a line, just like the British, to file out in an orderly way. Yes, we bombed in Buea, but consider this: we did about fifty concerts, workshops or jam sessions during thirty-six working days, so you could say the tour was ninety-eight percent successful."

Knowledge of American jazz is minimal. Even the students, if they had heard of Duke Ellington and Louis Armstrong, knew nothing of Charlie Parker or Lester Young. "Their conception of jazz, unfortunately, is James Brown and Otis Redding. Our music came as a surprise.

"For the first three weeks we spent all our spare time in nightclubs. Everything we heard was utterly alien to the ethnic music we expected. It wasn't authentic African and it wasn't jazz. In all those thousands of miles we didn't hear a single outstanding jazz musician. A couple of electric guitars here, a fender bass there. Finally we got to Dakar, Senegal, on the extreme western tip of the continent, which was very much like Oceanside, California, or San Diego. Dakar was the most advanced of all the cities—musically, too. We heard a cornetist who played in a strictly modal style, reminiscent of John Coltrane.''

Nelson says he ''never felt a draft'' despite anti-American news slanting which he sensed on some of the local radio stations. Africans who heard one side of the story through this medium and a different version from the Voice of America were confused. Their vision of the United States was reflected in their certainty that all the American musicians' instruments were solid gold; Nelson had difficulty convincing anyone they were made of brass.

By the same token, they wondered how a country so rich could be in so much turmoil. ''It's not true that they don't give a damn,'' says Nelson. ''They're very concerned with the black revolution, and they all manage to keep in touch, because even people who have no electricity can afford a tiny transistor radio. To my amazement, I would see the words 'Black Power' scraped in charcoal on a mud hut. But poverty is everywhere, and I foresee neither a social nor a musical revolution. There will be no significant jazz player coming out of Africa. I'm arranging for American record companies to put some African radio stations on their mailing lists, to send them LPs of men like Freddie Hubbard and Herbie Hancock so they'll feel a little more in touch.''

Racial attitudes colored the response to Nelson's musicians. ''Our trumpeter, Freddie Hill, would get a lot of applause before he even started to play, because he was black, the darkest member of the group. On the other hand, if they liked John Klemmer's saxophone solos, they would react just as warmly afterward, even though he's white.''

Frank Strozier, the blond, blue-eyed saxophonist who claims some African ancestry, was the subject of much ''Is he or isn't he?'' probing. ''Frank and I both got sick and tired of the constant questioning. I would say 'What does it matter if we're three whites and four Negroes or any other ratio. The guy's a great musician.' I'd tell them the blues is an American art form that derived from the shores of Africa, and that Frank was going to interpret the story of a journey, *Goin' to Chicago*. He got a standing ovation every time; in the final analysis the feeling he transmitted was all that mattered.''

Ouagadougou, Upper Volta, was the scene of the tour's only TV appearance. "They had three cameras and several capable African technicians, some of them trained at RCA in New York, but with those 5,000 watt lamps and no air conditioning we were about to perish."

Nelson feels that despite the presence of a minority of whites who hate Africa and the Africans, almost everyone he met in the Peace Corps or the Foreign Service had an enlightened attitude, including white as well as black United States ambassadors. He told one story that illustrated as much as any the impact of the musicians as goodwill envoys.

"When we arrived in Ft. Lamy, Chad, Ambassador Sheldon B. Vance said: 'We're hoping for a miracle.' I told him we'd do all we could, but he said, 'No, not from you. The president of the country is coming tonight. He's been annoyed lately to find that when he gets to an official function, half his ministers are absent. So there's a new drive on: 'everybody must be there before I arrive.'

"At the concert the turnout was just what the ambassador had hoped for. After the first set, the president of Chad asked to have his picture taken with me and the band. Ambassador Vance told us later, 'I think the door is now partly open, because of what you did .' He told us how happy he was that we would come to his little country and make his job a bit easier.

"If that's what music can do as the universal language, our mission was accomplished. Still what I remember best is those music-hungry people roaring for another encore. It was a tough trip, but I've been asked by the State Department if I'd like to go back some day, and you know what? I'd be happy to rough it again."   —MAY 1969

(Oliver Nelson spent most of the next seven years writing music for television, playing at U.S. and overseas jazz festivals, and stepping up his activities as a publisher of his own music. By 1975 he had not returned to Africa, nor had he made any more tours for the U.S. State Department.)

Oliver Nelson II

"If sometimes our great artists have been the most critical of our society, it is because their sensitivity and their concern for justice, which must motivate any true artist, makes them aware that our nation falls short of its highest potential. I see little of more importance to the future of our country and our civilization than full recognition of the place of the artist."
—John F. Kennedy, Oct. 26, 1963

These words were heard in *The Kennedy Dream*, a memorial album composed and conducted by Oliver Nelson. They preceded a movement in Nelson's suite, *The Artists' Rightful Place!* I was reminded of Kennedy's declaration, and of the music it inspired Nelson to write, when I heard the news that this gifted composer, this man of so many talents that there were not enough hours in the day to express them all adequately, had died of a heart attack at the age of 43 on October 28, 1975.

Oliver Nelson's music did not go entirely unrecognized. He was nominated four times for a Grammy (but never won); was voted best arranger several times in *Down Beat* Critics' and Readers' polls; won the Grand Gala du Disque award in Amsterdam for his memorable album, *Blues and the Abstract Truth*. He had the respect not only of the jazz community but of the commercial world of studio music in which he worked since his move to Los Angeles several years ago.

Yet there was a clear disparity in Nelson's life between accomplishment and aspirations. Talking to me and to others in recent months, he left an unmistakable impression of being torn by conflicting forces.

He was a generous, humanitarian and deeply dedicated man. Throughout his career he expressed himself passionately as a composer, arranger, conductor, educator and, because his love of playing remained deeply ingrained to the end, a brilliant alto saxophonist.

By Hollywood standards, he was successful, reaching millions of listeners with the underscoring for *Ironside, It Takes a Thief, Name of the Game, Matt Lincoln, Longstreet,* and *Six Million Dollar Man.*

The truth is that making durable music and making a living at music are too often incompatible. Oliver Nelson's problems in addressing himself to the inbuilt schizophrenia of the music business were symptomatic of a malaise prevalent among great composers during the past decade, and particularly among those raised in the jazz tradition of honest self-expression and integrity. More and more the artist finds himself caught in a web of demands that are at odds with his true ambitions. Time and again the work of exceptionally capable men is reduced to sadly obvious pitches for mass acceptance. Nelson did not want to pattern his life that way. Such suites as *Black, Brown and Beautiful,* no matter how limited the demand for them, were more fully representative of his beliefs and ideals than much of the music to which he gave himself in the past few years.

President Kennedy's comments on the artists' rightful place, their concern for justice, meant among other things justice for the artists themselves. If justice is done to the full oeuvre of Oliver Nelson, it will be done posthumously, in the form, as Langston Hughes would have said, of a dream deferred; and this is something that all of us who knew and admired Oliver will regret forever.   —NOVEMBER 1975

Mahalia Jackson's singing illustrated the close link between black religious music and blues.

Top jazz singer **Cleo Laine** has also starred in opera, musical comedy, and straight dramatic roles.
(Photo: V.J. Ryan)

Multi-instrumentalist **Yusef Lateef** received his Ph.D
in Music from the University of Massachusetts in
September 1975.

John Lewis, whose Modern Jazz Quartet was the most
widely-acclaimed small jazz group from the 1950s on.

Mel Lewis and **Thad Jones,** co-leaders of the 1970s' most successful big band.

Charles Lloyd, the popular young saxophonist of the late 1960s and early 1970s.

Marian McPartland's appearances include the fashionable East Side clubs of New York City; international jazz festivals; and college concerts. (Photo: Roy Bray)

Shelly Manne has played on numerous movie and TV sound-tracks, has been heard on more than a thousand LPs, and ran a popular jazz club in Los Angeles in the early 1970s.

Composer-arranger-pianist **Phil Moore** has accompanied Dorothy Dandridge and Lena Horne, coached Frank Sinatra, Marilyn Monroe and Goldie Hawn among others, and is active as a screenwriter and radio network composer.

197

Gerry Mulligan is busier than ever these days.
(Photo: David D. Spitzer)

198

Romano Mussolini, son of *Il Duce,* accomplished jazz pianist, has toured with Chet Baker and Caterina Valente. (Photo: Yani Begakis)

Anita O'Day in MGM's *The Outfit;* her style has influenced many singers in recent years.

Oliver Nelson and his State Department-sponsored group in Mali, West Africa, 1969. Left to right: Nelson, John Klemmer (tenor sax), Fred Hill (half-hidden, trumpet), Frank Strozier (alto sax), Bobby Morin (drums), Ernie Watts (reeds), Stan Gilbert (bass).

199

Joe Venuti, the fabled jazz violinist. (Photo: Stanley L. Payne)

Sarah Vaughan at the Hollywood Bowl,
summer 1974. (Photo: Michael Hyatt)

The People Who Live in the Village

The children's rooms were back to the way they were, but there was still no liveliness in the village.

And no wonder, since the people in the village had been erased too.

"I miss my mom," a boy said sadly.

"Next we'll draw everyone's family and the village's people!"

Rayon said, reaching up on her tiptoes to draw a round head.

"My mother and I have exactly the same hairstyle."

"My father wears smart-looking suits."

The children all called out the details about their parents.

"Were there a lot of people other than your family living here?"

"Draw the lady who bakes the cakes. I want to eat cake!"

"I have a cavity that's bothering me... I need to go see the dentist!"

"I miss the old lady who lives in my neighborhood!"

Let's draw the pictures
inside the frames

Let's draw curtains
fluttering in the breeze

Choose your favorite book
titles for the spines